Custer's Last Stand

On June 25, 1876, George Armstrong Custer led a small band of about two hundred U.S. Army men in an attack against an overwhelming force of Sioux and Cheyenne Indian warriors. The fierce battle, which was fought in the valley of the Little Bighorn River, is one of the best-known and most written-about campaigns in American military history. Why did Custer go into battle when his forces were so vastly outnumbered? Why did he disobey orders and attack before he had joined the rest of the 7th Cavalry units?

Custer's Last Stand is an exciting book about one of the most colorful and heartbreaking episodes in American history. Author Quentin Reynolds provides a vivid portrait of the controversial Custer—as a young cadet at West Point, as a Civil War hero who at the age of twenty-five became the youngest general in the army, and finally as a courageous but foolhardy Indian fighter in the Dakota Territory.

Custer's Last Stand

☆ ☆ ☆ ☆ ☆ ☆ ☆ ☆

By Quentin Reynolds

Random House ☆ New York

Library of Congress Cataloging-in-Publication Data:
Reynolds, Quentin James, 1902–1965.
  Custer's last stand.
  (A Landmark book)
  SUMMARY: A biography of the boy who not only saw his dream to be a general come true but also became the famous Indian fighter who led the attack against Crazy Horse and Sitting Bull at the Battle of the Little Bighorn. 1. Custer, George Armstrong, 1839–1876—Juvenile literature. 2. Little Bighorn, Battle of the, 1876—Juvenile literature. [1. Custer, George Armstrong, 1839–1876. 2. Little Bighorn, Battle of the, 1876] I. Title. E467.1.C99R4 1987 973.8'1'0924 [B] [92] 87-4650 ISBN: 0-394-89178-3 (trade); 0-394-90320-X (lib. bdg.)

Manufactured in the United States of America

1 2 3 4 5 6 7 8 9 0

CONTENTS

☆　　☆　　☆　　☆　　☆　　☆　　☆　　☆

Custer's
Last Stand

1

☆　☆　☆　☆　☆　☆　☆　☆

A BOY HAS A DREAM

When George Armstrong Custer was four years old, he had a dream, and less than twenty years later the dream came true. This is how it happened.

For his fourth birthday the boy's father, who was an officer in the militia, gave him a little soldier's suit as a present. It was an exact copy of the suit that Mr. Custer himself wore when he was drilling the troops of New Rumley.

New Rumley was a small town in Ohio, but the farmers and workmen from miles around had formed what they called the New Rumley Invincibles. Although the group numbered only about a hundred men, they took their drilling very seriously. There were rumors that there might be a war with Mexico. There were rumors, too, of Indian uprisings, for in 1843, Ohio was still a western frontier.

The children that George Armstrong Custer knew never called him George or Armstrong; his nickname was Autie, though to this day no one knows why. Even his mother and his big, husky father called him Autie, and years later the Indians would call him Autie when they were hunting him.

Every time the New Rumley Invincibles drilled, little Autie, his eyes bright with excitement, would watch them. When they went on marches, Autie would trail behind until his father's stern eye fell upon him. Then he would run home.

His father's name was Emanuel. Emanuel Custer was part English, part Dutch, and part German, but he thought of himself as being one hundred percent American.

Little Autie thought that his father was just

about the most wonderful man in the world. He could shoot better than anyone else; he could ride the wildest horse; he could outwrestle any farmer for miles around. Yet, with all of his great strength, he was soft-spoken and gentle. He was a stern father, but a just one. Above everything else he hated lying, and little Autie learned to hate it too.

Autie had bright golden hair and very pink cheeks. Yet no one ever called him sissy because of that. Even at four he was sturdy.

In those days a four-year-old son of a farmer had to help with the chores. Autie couldn't milk the cows, or cut the firewood, or help plow the land, but there were other things he could do. He could keep the wood box filled and he could weed the vegetable garden and he could sweep out the kitchen every day. Boys grew up quickly in those days, and they were given jobs to do that four-year-olds today are never given. There were no "hired hands" in the wilderness that was Ohio nearly one hundred and fifty years ago.

His mother, whose name was Marie, asked Autie what he wanted for his fourth birthday.

"A gun," he said promptly, "like Father's. A sword like Father's and a uniform like Father's."

"Well, we'll see," she said with a smile.

To tell the truth, she had already bought the boy's birthday present from a peddler who came around every few months with a pack on his back. She had bought him six pencils, some colored chalk, and a slate. They didn't have big blackboards in those days, but they did have small slates.

When Autie's father came home that night after drill, Marie told him what the boy wanted. "He's a silly boy," she said fondly. "Imagine a four-year-old wanting a gun, a sword, and a uniform."

"Well"—Emanuel Custer was a little embarrassed—"I guess any four-year-old boy would want a gun. . . ."

"Emanuel," she said sharply, "don't tell me that you've gone and bought him anything foolish like that."

"Not exactly, Marie," he answered slowly. "But you know the boy is only happy when he watches us drill. So . . . well . . . to tell you the truth," he blurted out, "I did get him a little gun. It's made out of wood," he added hastily as he saw the look of fright in her eyes. "I had the carpenter make it up. And he made a little wooden sword, too. Then I had our company tailor make Autie a little uniform. Just wait till you see it."

Marie went a little pale. She hated war, she hated fighting. But she realized that her son would be growing up soon. One day he might have to exchange his wooden gun for a real one and take his place among the men who guarded the little settlement from Indian raids.

"The boy has to grow up sometime," Emanuel said gently, and Marie nodded.

She was a pioneer woman, used to the hard life of the frontier. And she trusted her big husband's judgment. Even when he was very young, he had known the right thing to do. While he was still a boy, he had worked as a blacksmith, and he still had a blacksmith's big hands. The muscles of his arms stood out like tight cords. Emanuel had been a good blacksmith too—so good that he had made enough money to buy this farm in the forest outside of New Rumley, where they now lived.

Autie's birthday was December 5, not a very good time to have a birthday. It was too close to Christmas. Autie's mother wisely put the pencils, the colored chalk, and the slate away. She'd save these for a Christmas present.

When little Autie awoke on the morning of his birthday, he ran to the wood box, grabbed a log, and threw it on the smoldering fire, which had almost died during the night. The Custers' home was really a cabin, and the only heat came from the big open fireplace. It was Autie's job to start the fire every morning. The bright flames lit up the room (it was only four in the morning and still dark). There, on the chair beside the bed, was a gun, a sword, and a uniform.

Autie's eyes sparkled with joy when he saw his birthday present. He really hadn't expected anything like this. He threw off his heavy woolen pajamas and put on the uniform. It fit perfectly. It was dark blue and had little brass buttons on it. The hat was best of all. It was a sombrero—the mark of a cavalry man. He put on the hat with fingers that trembled. He hooked the little wooden sword to his belt and held the gun in his hands.

No one else was awake yet. Autie's mother and father were still asleep. There was no one around to whom he could show off his uniform, his sword, and his gun. His brother, David, and his sisters, Ann and Lydia, were asleep upstairs.

Autie sat on his bed, fingering the toy gun, pointing it at imaginary Indians. Then he put the gun down and waved his little sword. He pretended that he was leading a troop of cavalry. And then, believe it or not, he fell asleep!

An hour later his mother and father got up. They dressed and came into the big room which served as kitchen, dining room, and bedroom. There was Autie sound asleep, dressed in his uniform, his gun and his sword by his side.

"He may sleep many nights like that," his father said gravely. "Out on the plains, deep in the woods. It's a good lesson for a boy to learn—to sleep with his gun at his side."

Marie Custer bowed her head in sorrow for a moment, but she knew that her husband probably spoke the truth. "If he has to be a soldier," she said, "I pray that he will be a good one."

"I'm a general." A whisper came from the sleeping boy. "I'm a general," he repeated, and even as he slept his face was shining with excitement.

"He's dreaming," Autie's mother said quietly. And then little Autie's eyes opened. He blinked to get the sleep out of them. He sat up and looked at his father. Then, very solemnly, he said, "Father, I had a dream. I dreamed that I was a general."

He brandished his little sword and said excitedly, "Someday I'm going to be a general. Someday I'm going to ride a big white horse and fight the Indians. . . ."

"Maybe," his father said softly to Marie, "our boy was born to be a leader of men."

2

☆　☆　☆　☆　☆　☆　☆　☆

AUTIE GOES TO SCHOOL

By the time that Autie Custer was ten, he had three younger brothers: Nevin, who was seven; Thomas, four; and Boston (whom he called Bos), who was a year old. But Autie's best friend was a boy named Charles Buckley, who lived in Monroe, Michigan.

Monroe seemed a long way off from New

Rumley because there were no railroads then in that part of the country, and no real roads. There were only country roads and trails. Autie's sister Lydia made her home in Monroe with her husband, David Reed. She lived in a big house, and because she had no children of her own, the big house seemed lonely. Lydia had always loved golden-haired Autie, and she persuaded her mother to let the boy stay with her.

Autie's mother was very, very busy with her three little boys, so she agreed, but her real reason for allowing her son to stay with Lydia was the very fine school in Monroe. There was only a little one-room schoolhouse in New Rumley.

Marie Custer was afraid that her son Autie was growing up wild. He roamed the woods like an Indian, and he knew the name of every tree and plant in the wilderness.

When he wasn't in the woods, Autie was with the New Rumley Invincibles, listening eagerly to their stories of Indian fights. He would borrow books from them, and the books were always books about fighting. He wasn't very good at spelling, but he could tell you the names of every one of the American generals who had fought in the war against Mexico which had just ended. He couldn't do long division very well, but he could go through the manual of arms like a veteran.

When one of his father's friends would say, "What do you want to be when you grow up, Autie?" he'd always give the same answer.

"I'm going to be a general," he would say firmly.

His mother thought that Stebbins Academy in Monroe would knock that sort of nonsense out of his head. So she decided to send him to Monroe for a while. When she told him, he was wild with excitement.

"Frenchtown!" Autie cried. "I've always wanted to go there."

"Frenchtown?" his mother said, puzzled. "Not Frenchtown, Autie—Monroe."

"It used to be Frenchtown, Mother," he said earnestly. "Honestly it was. Way back in 1813 it was named Frenchtown because it was settled by Frenchmen. Didn't you ever hear of the Battle of Raisin River?"

"No, darling, I never did."

"Well, Mother"—Autie was proud to show off his knowledge—"it was in 1813 and the Indians under Tecumseh crossed the Raisin River and attacked the settlement. They came at night and surprised the Kentucky mounted riflemen who were there to defend Frenchtown. The Indians stampeded the horses and, well, a mounted ri-fleman isn't much good if he hasn't a horse. You know that."

"Yes, I know that, son," she said, trying not to appear worried. Did her boy ever think of anything but soldiering and fighting?

"And the Indians massacred those soldiers," Autie said solemnly. "They called it the Battle of Raisin River. General Proctor was in charge of the Kentucky riflemen. He made a big mistake, Mother. He thought the river would protect him. He never thought the Indians would cross the river, but they did. I'll never make that mistake. When you fight Indians, you have to protect your right and left flanks. You have to guard against surprise. You have—"

"How do you know these things, Autie?" Mrs. Custer asked, a little pale now. She had a strange feeling that her boy was growing up too fast, and a strange feeling that he would never be satisfied until he was a soldier.

"I listen to the men in Father's troop," he said simply. "I know about every Indian fight in this part of the country, Mother."

"Well," she said weakly, "there are no Indians in Frenchtown . . . I mean Monroe . . . now. Monroe is a big city, and it's civilized and quiet and it has a wonderful school."

Everything she said about Monroe was true. The only city in the state bigger than Monroe was Detroit. And Stebbins Academy was a wonderful school.

So off Autie went to live with his sister Lydia Reed and to attend Stebbins Academy.

At the school the boys were seated alphabetically, two to a desk. Charles Buckley was the last of the *B*'s and Autie was the only boy in the class whose last name began with *C*, so these two boys found themselves sitting side by side. They looked each other over warily.

Charles had been at the school for two years, and he felt very superior to this boy from far-off Ohio. Autie sat there, his eyes looking down at the top of the desk. Charles wondered if he was scared. He said to himself in disgust, "Why, he looks more like a girl than a boy, with that golden hair. And he's even afraid to raise his eyes." He looked at Autie again and was surprised to see Autie's left eyelid lower in a faint but unmistakable wink.

Charles was puzzled. Why was he winking? Then he heard a scraping noise. He looked down and saw that the new boy had a knife in his right hand and the knife was scratching two initials in the soft wood of the desk. Charles was fascinated by the quick, sure movements of the knife in the slender but strong fingers of the new boy.

Mr. Stebbins was calling the roll. "Charles Buckley," he called, and Charles said "Present." Then Mr. Stebbins called, "George Armstrong Custer," and the new boy said "Present" calmly, but his knife kept on cutting into the desk. By the time Mr. Stebbins had finished calling the roll, the new boy had finished. He leaned back to let Charles see his work. There, plain to see, were the initials A.C.

Charles shook his head. He didn't understand. He had just heard Mr. Stebbins call out "George Armstrong Custer." Why did the new boy carve the initials A.C.? His first name did not begin with *A*.

Finally it was time for recess, and the whole class swarmed joyously outside. Charles Buckley was at Autie's side.

"What does A.C. mean?" he asked.

"Autie Custer, that's my name," the new boy said.

"I thought it was George Armstrong Custer," Charles said.

"Nobody ever called me anything but Autie," the new boy said. "Even my father and the men of the New Rumley Invincibles call me Autie."

"What are the New Rumley Invincibles?" Charles asked.

"Indian fighters," Autie said casually. Well, it was half true. If New Rumley were ever attacked, they were the ones who would have to fight the Indians. "My father is their officer," Autie said proudly. "And someday I'll take his place. After I get out of West Point, I mean."

"West Point!" Charles gasped. Almost every great American general had been a West Point man. In those days boys didn't have baseball players or movie stars for their heroes. Their idols were the men who had led the fight against Mexico, the officers who had fought the Indians; and these were all West Pointers.

The other boys came up now to look over the newcomer. They had to make up their minds about him. Would they accept him or not? Autie stood there, smiling a little. He wasn't a bit bothered by their stares.

"Maybe you'd like to try my knife," he said to Charles. He handed the knife to him.

"It has three blades," Charles said in amazement. "I've never seen one like this."

"They call it a jackknife," Autie explained. "The blades fold right into the handle. That's to keep the blades from getting rusty. And if one blade breaks, why, you still have two more. When you live in Indian country, you can't be too careful of your knife. Never know when you'll need it," Autie said solemnly.

"Can I try it?" asked the biggest boy in the school.

"Sure," Autie told him. "You can all try it. But watch out, it's real sharp."

"Sharp? You bet it is," said Charles Buckley, and he laughed. "You should have seen Autie carve his initials in the desk while Old Man Stebbins was calling the roll."

They looked at Autie with respect. They forgot his golden hair and his pink cheeks. Anyone who could carve his initials in a desk without Mr. Stebbins catching him at it was pretty clever.

From that moment on Autie Custer was one of them; within a month he was their leader. No one knew just how it had come about. But there was something about Autie Custer that was different. He didn't talk loudly; he didn't bully kids smaller than himself; he didn't give orders; yet they all followed him. Yes, there was something about him. . . .

His father probably knew what it was when he had said, "Maybe our boy was born to be a leader."

3

☆　　☆　　☆　　☆　　☆　　☆　　☆　　☆

THE BOY WHO HATED HOMEWORK

There was one thing Autie hated above everything else—homework. But luckily for him, he had a wonderful memory. He could hear Mr. Stebbins name the states (there were only thirty in 1848) and he would never forget them. But he still hated homework.

He liked to read much better, and the books he

read were always stories of Indian fighting. Sometimes he would bring one of the books to school with him. When it came time for the geography lesson, he'd take out his big geography, open it, and bend over it very seriously. But he usually had one of his books hidden in the geography. When Mr. Stebbins thought Autie was tracing the course of the Mississippi River, he was really far, far away with the great Indian fighters of the day.

You could fool Mr. Stebbins for a while, but not forever. Mr. Stebbins knew all about Autie's amazing memory; he knew that the boy was getting by in his lessons because of it. One day he kept him in after school for a talk.

"What do you want to be when you grow up, Autie?" he asked.

"A soldier," Autie replied. "I want to go to West Point and then become a general."

"That's a good ambition, Autie," the principal said gravely. "But it isn't easy to get into West Point."

"A congressman appoints you, doesn't he?" Autie asked.

"All a congressman can do is recommend you," Mr. Stebbins said. "Then you have to take an examination."

"You do?" Autie was amazed at that.

19

"Yes, and they examine you in every subject. You are very good in history, Autie, and fair at geography. But you can't spell, and as for arithmetic, well, you aren't very good at it, are you?"

Autie shook his head. "No, but I can stay in the woods without getting lost, and I can march for two days if I have to, and sleep on the ground, and I can ride a horse bareback, and—"

"They don't ask you about such things when you take the West Point examination. Arithmetic is important to a soldier. Always remember that, Autie. They examine you very thoroughly on that subject."

"How does arithmetic help a soldier?" Autie asked scornfully.

Mr. Stebbins explained to him how you figure out the range of a big gun. You don't just aim a cannon at the enemy and fire it. The enemy is far away; you can't even see him. You find out where the enemy is and then figure out how much powder to put in your cannon to land the shot at the right spot. You do this by using arithmetic in its highest form.

Mr. Stebbins told Autie about mapmaking, too, and how important it was to a soldier. You had to figure out how high the ground was on the battlefield, and that was also done by arithmetic.

Then, suppose you were an observer. Maybe they would send you up in a balloon, as they sent observers up in balloons during the Mexican War. When the balloon came down, you would have to make a report of what you had seen. The commanding officer would ask, "How many infantry did you see? How many big guns? How many horses? How many tents were there?" He might ask all kinds of questions like that, so you would need to be able to count quickly and accurately.

"If you want to go to West Point, Autie, you must pay more attention to homework," Mr. Stebbins said. "With your memory, it shouldn't be hard."

This came as very much of a shock to Autie Custer. He had never thought that a soldier did anything but ride a horse, wave a sword, and shoot a gun. Arithmetic? None of the New Rumley Invincibles knew anything about arithmetic. But then, he had to admit to himself, none of the New Rumley Invincibles was a West Point graduate; none of them was a general.

Autie walked home with Charles Buckley and told him what Mr. Stebbins had said. From now on, he told Charles, he would do his homework, all right, especially his arithmetic. And he did— for a while. But he just hated to study, and there was so much else to do. He was the best wrestler in school now, and the fastest runner.

Sometimes, when the woods called him, Autie would forget to study. He'd walk through the wilderness outside of Monroe stalking imaginary Indians, climbing a high tree to scout the land ahead, carefully bending branches and making marks on trees to give him a clear trail home. He was a real western boy, and he hated to stay indoors.

Loving his sister as much as he did, Autie actually enjoyed doing farm chores to help her. He had learned to chop wood, and he was developing the strong arm muscles of his father.

During Autie's stay with his sister, she had a baby boy whom she named Armstrong, after him, but he immediately nicknamed the baby Autie. Soon everyone was calling them Big Autie and Little Autie. It was strange to see the husky, golden-haired Autie playing with the baby; playing gently so as not to hurt him.

Sometimes, when the baby cried, Lydia would hear Autie say soothingly, "Don't cry. When you and I grow up, we'll go out West and fight Indians."

Each summer, when school was out, Autie hurried home to New Rumley. There was a new baby there now, another sister, named Margaret.

Autie was twelve when he went home for the third summer, and his mother looked at him in amazement. He was strong, and although he still had his golden hair, his face was freckled and he looked older than his years.

Now he could tramp in the fields with his father and help him bring in the crops, and he could milk a cow and ride the farm horse bareback.

One day Autie's father asked him good-naturedly, "What did they teach you at that school?"

"History and geography and arithmetic," Autie replied. "But I'm not much good at arithmetic."

"Then you'd better forget about West Point," his father said casually.

Autie looked up, surprised. "That's what Mr. Stebbins told me. He said I'd have to take an examination in arithmetic to get into West Point."

"That's right, son. You know, if you ever got lost in the woods, arithmetic would help you."

"How?" This was hard to believe.

"If you know how, you can look at the sun and figure what time it is," Mr. Custer told Autie. "Then you take a bearing or two and you'll know which is north, south, east, and west. Once you know how to figure those things out, you'll never get lost in the woods."

Autie looked very downcast. "But you never studied arithmetic, Father," he said. "And you can do all those things."

"That's right," his father said gravely. "But it took me a lifetime to learn. You can learn it all in a few short years at school."

"I have only one more year to go at Stebbins Academy," Autie said.

"I've been thinkin' about that," Emanuel Custer said slowly. "As long as you're still so set on going to West Point, we have to make plans. Now, I hear there's a real good school over in Monroe called the Seminary. The Reverend Boyd is principal, and they tell me he's very good."

"We know all about the Seminary," Autie said gloomily. "It's very hard. They give you two hours of homework every night."

His father nodded and said, "Yes, I hear it's real hard. Not as hard as West Point, but real hard. Maybe you'd better forget the whole idea. You just finish at Stebbins and come back here on the farm with me."

"But I want to be a soldier!" Autie cried.

"If you want it bad enough, you'll have to work for it. You don't get anything for nothing in this life, Autie. God helps those who help themselves. Who were the two big heroes of the Mexican War?"

"General Taylor and General Scott," Autie answered promptly.

"That's right, son. And they had to learn a lot before they were made officers. It wasn't easy, but they really wanted to be generals, and they worked at it."

"I want to be a general too," Autie said firmly.

"I can make a good farmer out of you, son, but I can't make a good general out of you. You've got to choose now. What'll it be, the farm or the Seminary?"

"The Seminary," Autie said.

4

☆　☆　☆　☆　☆　☆　☆　☆

AUTIE GROWS UP . . .

It was called Boyd's Seminary, and the Reverend Boyd was quite different from the easygoing Mr. Stebbins. The Reverend Boyd knew that the country was growing up and that it would need leaders. He was determined to produce some of these leaders. That first year was terrible for Autie. The Reverend Boyd knew about the boy's ambition to go to West Point, and he made up his mind to prepare Autie so that if he ever got the chance, he could pass the examination. But Autie just wasn't a natural student.

He could remember the capitals of every state in the Union without any trouble, but give him a simple problem in long division and he was in trouble. However, the Reverend Boyd kept working with him, and at least Autie passed everything his first year.

The second year was really hard, because now the class took up algebra and geometry. Sometimes after school Autie would walk home with his head down, completely discouraged. His path home led him by the house of Monroe's leading citizen, Judge Daniel S. Bacon.

Judge Bacon was more than a judge. He was president of the Monroe Bank, a director of the first Michigan railroad, and he owned about half the town of Monroe. Everyone had a lot of respect for Judge Bacon.

As Autie went by the Bacon house one day, he heard a voice cry out, "Hello, you Custer boy!" Autie looked up and blinked. He was looking at the prettiest girl he had ever seen. She was leaning over the white fence in front of the house.

"Who—who—who are you?" he stammered.

"I'm Elizabeth Bacon," she said calmly. "But

everybody calls me Libbie." Then she turned around and fled into the house.

Autie stood there for a moment. He had never seen a girl quite like this one before. There was something different about her. She talked straight out like a boy. But why had she run away?

"When I'm a general I bet she won't run away," Autie said to himself.

It was a long, long time before he saw her again, but every now and then he found himself thinking of her.

At the end of the second year Autie graduated from the Seminary. Boyd's Seminary would be called a prep school or a private high school today. There were no public high schools in Monroe in those days.

Autie was sixteen now, but no nearer to West Point and to being a general than he had been the day he was given a uniform for his fourth birthday. He had not done too well at school. He had just managed to pass everything.

The Reverend Boyd called him in for a talk. He liked this Custer boy, but he was a bit worried about him. The boy just wouldn't discipline himself, just wouldn't force himself to study. And he wanted to go to West Point.

"Autie," he said gravely, "you're sixteen now. What have you decided to do?"

"I don't know," Autie replied. "I want to go to West Point, but even if a congressman recommended me, I couldn't pass the examinations."

"That's true, Autie," the principal said, "but I have an idea. You look older than your age—you look eighteen. How would you like to be a teacher?"

Autie looked up in amazement. "A teacher?" he cried. "How would that help me pass my examinations to West Point? Besides, I don't know anything. I couldn't teach anybody . . ."

"Wait a minute, Autie," and the Reverend Boyd smiled. "Not so fast. There is a little school over at New Athens in Ohio, not too far from New Rumley. They need a teacher over there and they've asked me to recommend one. One thing about you—at least," he said dryly, looking at the strong boy, "you could keep order in school."

"But I don't want to be a teacher!" Autie cried. "I want to be a soldier."

The principal nodded. "I know. But if you would teach for a year or two, you'd have a lot of spare time. You could spend that time studying. I'd give you the books you'd need. You must learn your algebra and geometry better before you can think of the West Point examination. The teaching wouldn't be hard. You'd have the youngest students, and even you know enough arithmetic to add and subtract."

Autie smiled. "This is the last thing I ever thought of," he said.

"Your father is a pretty wonderful man," the Reverend Boyd said. "He's paid for your education now for nearly five years. I think it's about time you started paying. The salary for teaching at New Athens is twenty-five dollars a month and your board. You could support yourself on that and even send a little money home. And you could study by yourself and master algebra and geometry. I have a funny idea about you, Autie."

"What's that?" Autie asked.

The Reverend Boyd got up and began to stride up and down the office. He was trying to pick the right words, because he felt that the whole course of Autie Custer's life might be altered by this little talk.

"You don't like to be told to study, Autie. You don't like what we call discipline, and your teachers and I haven't been able to teach you discipline. My idea is that you might be able to teach yourself something we can't teach you. If you're alone in New Athens with nobody to give you homework, with nobody to nag you—why, you might just say to yourself, 'I'm growing up.

I don't need somebody to tell me when to study or when to work. I'm old enough to decide for myself. I want to go to West Point. I'm old enough to realize I have to study to get to West Point. So I'll study.' "

The Reverend Boyd stopped. He didn't say anything for a while. Neither did Autie. Autie just stood there, considering the idea. He liked what the principal had said. The Reverend Boyd was right, he decided. He did hate to be told things, but by gosh, he could do things without being told.

"You have to choose now, Autie," the Reverend Boyd said. "You can go back and work on the farm with your father, or you can go to West Point. But you need at least a full year of study before you can take that examination. You've got to choose, Autie."

"That's just what Father said," Autie thought. "They're both right. I have to choose. Nobody else can choose for me. Nobody else can live my life or study for me."

"I'll go to New Athens and teach for a year," Autie said quietly, and in that moment the course of his life was settled.

He went home and spent the summer on the farm. It was a wonderful summer. His little brothers were growing up. They were big enough to go into the woods with him. He gave his jack-knife to Tommy, who was always his favorite. Lydia wasn't there, but his older sister Ann was, and he loved her very much.

The summer passed all too quickly, and when September came he found himself standing before a class at the Beech Point School at nearby New Athens. The pupils looked at him in amazement. He certainly didn't look like a teacher.

Autie smiled at the boys and they smiled right back. He had the knack of making everyone like him, and that was a handy knack for a teacher to have. Remembering that he had been a pupil himself only a few short weeks ago, he was understanding with his charges. At the end of the first month he was paid twenty-five dollars. He rushed home to find his mother sitting in her favorite rocking chair. He put the money in her lap.

"It's the first money I ever earned," he said breathlessly, "and I want you to have it."

Then he hurried back to school.

He didn't really like teaching. He had always hated to stay indoors. Yet every time he thought of quitting, he saw the big gray battlements of West Point in his imagination and he kept on. He studied every night, and because no one was nagging him into it, he didn't mind it so much.

"Don't let your memory play you false," the Reverend Boyd had warned him just before he had left Monroe. "In geometry you can memorize a theorem easily enough, but merely memorizing it isn't understanding it. It isn't enough to say, 'A straight line is the shortest distance between two points.' You have to understand *why* it is the shortest distance. Don't just memorize your mathematics—understand it."

For one whole year and a good part of another Autie taught school and studied by himself. He had not only grown physically, he had grown mentally, too.

He went through the algebra and geometry books much more quickly than he had expected. Autie never did anything halfway. When he played, he played hard. Now that he had made up his mind to study, he studied hard. He studied so hard he ran right out of the books the Reverend Boyd had given him.

To see if he could borrow some new and more advanced books, he went to the McNeely Normal School at nearby Hopedale. Mr. Israel Carpenter, the principal of the school, listened to Autie's story.

"Of course you may borrow our books," said Mr. Carpenter, impressed by the enthusiasm of the young teacher. "But we can do more than that. We hold classes here in the late afternoon, so that the farmers' sons can come in to school after their morning's work is done. You're free in the afternoons. Why not enroll here as a student? Some of our teachers are familiar with the type of examination West Point gives, and they'll give you special help."

Autie's eyes lit up. A few months ago he had hated school. Now here he was, happy because he was to be allowed to attend classes again. So he immediately enrolled in the McNeely Normal School. It was the wisest decision he ever made in his life. He found studying easy now—because he wanted to study. And finally he felt he was ready for the West Point examination.

But first he had to have the recommendation of his congressman. He asked his father about that.

"Trouble is, Autie," his father said, scratching his head thoughtfully, "that Congressman John Bingham, who is the congressman from our district, is a Republican and I'm a Democrat."

"If you're a Democrat, then I'm a Democrat," Autie said loyally. He didn't really know the difference between a Democrat and a Republican. Autie never cared about politics.

"Congressman Bingham is a mighty fine man,

even if he and I don't agree on politics," Emanuel Custer said. "Maybe you'd better write to him anyway."

"I'll write to him today," Autie said promptly.

5

☆　☆　☆　☆　☆　☆　☆　☆

. . . AND BECOMES A CADET

The letter Autie wrote to Congressman John Bingham showed that he had been studying English as well as algebra. It was really a wonderful letter for so young a boy to have written. It said:

Hopedale, Ohio, May 27th, 1856

TO THE HON. JOHN A. BINGHAM.

SIR:—Wishing to learn something in relation to the matter of appointment of cadets to the West Point Military Academy, I have taken the liberty of addressing you on the subject. My only apology for thus intruding on your notice is, that I cannot obtain such information here. And as the matter is to be finally settled in Washington, I have thought better to make application at headquarters from the beginning. If . . . you can find time to inform me as to the necessary qualifications for admission, and if our congressional district is unrepresented there or not, or at least when there will be a vacancy, you will confer a great favor on me.

I am desirous of going to West Point, and I think my age and tastes would be in accordance with its requirements. But I must forbear on that for the present. I am now in attendance at the McNeely Normal School in Hopedale, and could obtain from the principal, if necessary, testimonials of moral character. I would also say that I have the consent of my parents in the course which I have in view. Wishing to hear from you as soon as convenient,

I remain,
Yours respectfully,
G. A. CUSTER

Autie mailed the letter to far-off Washington and waited impatiently for an answer. It came a month later, and it was very discouraging. A boy had already been selected from the district for that year, but the congressman said he'd keep Autie in mind for the next year's recommendation.

A whole year to wait! Autie felt that the world had come to an end. Was it really worth the effort? He clenched his fists, tightened his jaw, and said to himself, "You bet it's worth the effort. I can never be a general unless I go to West Point." So back to the classroom he went. Teaching and studying. Teaching and studying—that's all he did now.

A few months after this, Congressman Bingham came to New Rumley to make a speech. Autie determined to see him. When the congressman had finished, Autie made his way through the crowd until he reached the congressman's side.

"My name is George Armstrong Custer, sir," he began. "You don't know who I am, but I wrote to—"

"Of course I know who you are, son," Congressman Bingham said, smiling. "I remember your letter well. It was a fine letter, and I think you'd make a fine cadet. Just be patient, son. I said I'd consider you for the next appointment, and now that I've met you, my boy, I must say you look as if you have the makings of a soldier in you. Even though"—his eyes twinkled—"you're the son of a Democrat. But we need Democrats in the army as well as Republicans, son. I won't forget you."

"Thank you, sir," Autie said in a daze. So this was a congressman. Why, he was like anyone else.

The congressman went to a meeting of the New Rumley Invincibles later that day. He went right up to Emanuel Custer, shook his hand, and said, "That's quite a boy you have there. Best looking kid I ever saw. He's really set on being a soldier, isn't he?"

"He aims higher than that, Congressman. Ever since he was four years old, he's wanted to be a general," Autie's father said.

Congressman Bingham laughed. "I never saw a general with golden hair, but it's what lies under the scalp that counts, not what is on top of it. Mr. Custer, I'd consider it a privilege to recommend your son to the West Point authorities. You can call that a promise."

"If you're not careful, you'll make a Republican out of me yet," Emanuel Custer said.

"Maybe between us, and with some help from

West Point, we can make a general out of the boy," the congressman said. Then he added, "I have a hunch—just one of those hunches a man gets now and then—that someday I'm going to be proud of helping your son become an officer."

During the fall and winter Autie worked hard. He divided his time between the Beech Point School, the McNeely Normal School, and the farm. After studying long hours, he felt good grabbing an axe and chopping enough logs to fill the same old wood box that still stood beside the kitchen stove.

By now the New Rumley Invincibles had raised enough money to buy horses and become a cavalry group. The men allowed Autie to ride the horses whenever he wished. Sometimes they would pick up a rather wild stallion, too hard-mouthed or stubborn for its owner to handle. Autie loved to get a horse of this type. He felt that he understood horses.

"Let me have any horse for two weeks and I'll break him," he used to say, and he wasn't boasting. He did understand horses, and horses seemed to like him.

So the winter passed, and one day (February 11, 1857) a long, official-looking letter arrived from Washington. With trembling hands Autie opened it. It was a letter from Congressman

Bingham telling him that he had received the appointment and that he must report to West Point for his entrance examinations in six weeks.

Autie was too filled with emotion to speak. He just handed the letter to his father. Emanuel Custer read it aloud. Then he put his arm around his son's shoulder.

"You always said you'd be a general," he said quietly. "I never doubted it, son. I don't doubt it now. You'll pass the examinations all right. I'm . . . I'm proud of you, Autie."

"If it hadn't been for you, Father, I never would have stuck it out at school," Autie said, his eyes shining. "I guess . . . guess I have the best father in the world."

Autie's mother hadn't said a word. Now she looked up, smiled, and said softly, "You *have* the best father in the world, Autie."

"I'll never forget it," Autie said. "Six weeks! Only six weeks left! Know what I'm going to do? I'm going to spend that whole six weeks at Normal School studying. Now I've really got something to study for. I'm even going to learn the mathematics they give you during the first year at West Point. I can't afford to fail those exams."

No one except the teachers at McNeely Normal School saw anything of Autie during the next five weeks. They were proud of this student who was so hungry for knowledge. Nobody from New Rumley had ever gone to West Point. Everyone wanted to help young Autie, but he listened only to the teachers. Geometry? Algebra? He knew those subjects by heart now. He not only knew them, he understood them. What was next? Trigonometry?

He couldn't even pronounce the word at first. But he knew that trigonometry was used by artillery officers to fix enemy positions, so he plunged right into it. While he was about it, he also learned some chemistry. As soon as he mastered one textbook he looked for another.

"You'll make it, Autie," Mr. Carpenter said quietly one day. "Now you just forget about studying this last week. Borrow a horse and ride through the woods. Get the cobwebs out of your brain. Get out on the farm with your father. Do your muscles good."

Autie took Mr. Carpenter's advice. A week out in the open did wonders for him. When he finally left for West Point, he was rested in mind and hard of body. He already carried himself like a soldier, although his golden hair didn't look very warlike. He arrived at West Point early one morning. The examinations began in the afternoon. He bent over the examination papers.

Why, these were questions he had been asked

before. Mr. Stebbins had once asked him some of these; the Reverend Boyd had asked him others, and Mr. Carpenter still others. Autie felt warm and grateful as his pencil hurried on, giving the answers in the neat handwriting Mr. Stebbins had once taught him. When he finished he knew that he had passed.

And he was right. A month later he entered West Point. For the next year he would be Plebe Custer.

The dream was beginning to come true.

6

☆　☆　☆　☆　☆　☆　☆　☆

AUTIE,
THE PLEBE

Experience has taught our military leaders that the first lesson a soldier must learn is discipline. In war, lives are saved when soldiers obey orders quickly without thinking. That was true in World War I; it was true in World War II; and it was true back in 1857.

Autie Custer at seventeen was slender but tall

and strong. His golden hair was unruly, and because he hated to waste time getting a haircut, it was usually too long. His eyes were dark blue, and only a few freckles remained on his cheeks. He was eager, confident, enthusiastic. For two years he had been his own boss. That's what he liked.

Now he was thrown into a little world of its own. He was a plebe, and at West Point a plebe is the lowest form of life known. A plebe has to salute every upperclassman he meets. He has to address every upperclassman as "sir." He has to do anything they order him to do. In 1857 a plebe lived in a small room with four other plebes. The floor was their bed, and each plebe had one blanket.

At first Autie was shocked by the discipline. The plebe lived by the drum or the bugle. He was drummed up in the morning; drummed to breakfast; bugled to classes and meals; and then drummed to bed. Anyone who didn't like the hard life was told to get out.

The commandant of West Point called the plebes together to tell them the rules. They all gathered in the big mess hall and stood at attention while he spoke.

"You come from different walks of life," he began. "Some of you are from rich New York families. Some are from Harvard or Yale. Others of you are the sons of farmers. Some of you have had easy lives. Others have had hard lives. Your life here will be hard, and some of you will fall by the wayside. You will be ordered to do many things you think to be foolish. You will be here for five full years. [Later, the West Point course was changed to four years.]

"But always remember," he added, "our business is to make officers of you. When you are an officer, you will be responsible for the safety of the men under you, and to keep them safe you must have discipline. How can you learn to command others unless you have first been commanded? When things get especially hard, remember that every great general you ever heard of went through the same thing here at West Point. Accept our rules, abide by them, and you will one day be an officer in the United States Army.

"There is unrest in the land today," he went on solemnly, "and there are war clouds in the sky. Our country needs officers—good officers—and if you abide by our rules, hard as they seem to you, we can promise you one thing. We promise that when you graduate from West Point, you will be a good officer."

Many times during the first year Autie, discouraged, enraged at what he thought to be the senseless commands of upperclassmen, was on the point of quitting. He still hated to take orders. But every time he fell into the depths of despair, the picture of his father came to mind.

"You always said you'd be a general. I never doubted it, son," his father had said. Well, he couldn't let his father down now. And perhaps the commandant was right. Perhaps this was the only way to become a good officer. Again he'd bend over the trigonometry book or the textbook on integral calculus. These were hard subjects to master, but his instructors emphasized how important they were to an artillery officer.

The dreary months devoted only to study and to discipline and to drilling crept on. But always there was the promise of the summer camp. Every plebe was longing to get out of the barracks and under a tent. Gradually the awkward plebes were beginning to look like soldiers, to march like soldiers.

Autie was popular with the other plebes. He smiled readily and he was good-natured. When they were ordered on a long march, he was always the freshest of all when they trooped back to the barracks. Then finally came June.

In June at West Point the three upper classes go home for a summer vacation, which is called a furlough, just as vacations are called in the army. But the first- and second-year men remain at West Point for the whole summer. However, they do get out of the barracks and into tents.

During Autie's first summer, he and the others pitched their tents on the plain northeast of West Point. There were eight rows of tents. There were six guard tents, and the cadets (they could call themselves cadets now instead of plebes) took turns on sentry duty. Each boy was on duty two hours, off four hours, on two hours, off four hours, and so forth.

There were no books, no study in the encampment. The duties of the cadets were now for the first time wholly military. They spent long hours drilling, and soon reached the perfection that only West Pointers can attain. They had hours of rifle practice.

Autie's eyes were constantly shining with excitement. This is why he had come to West Point. He felt that now he was really learning to be a soldier. He had to admit that the drudgery of study was necessary, but he hated it. He even hated to remain indoors for any length of time.

The officers in charge at the encampment never mentioned the word *democracy*, but the cadets were learning the meaning of the word every day. They lived close to one another—the rich, the poor, the banker's son, the orphan, the boy from Kentucky, and the lad from Boston. At first each had thought the accent of the others strange. A boy from New England could hardly understand the slow drawl of a cadet from the South. But gradually each began to understand the others; each realized that he and his part of the country were only tiny parts of the whole United States.

They learned that in time of war they would share a common danger. Now they were learning to share their common heritage of democracy. The discipline, the hard work, these were the price one paid for the great privilege of living in a democracy. The country itself was giving them a great education. It was giving them books, fine food, and a place to live. All this didn't cost the parents of the cadets a penny.

For the first time, Autie Custer realized what it meant to be an American. Back home his whole world consisted of New Rumley and Monroe. Now he realized how big the country really was. He realized, too, that boys whose fathers had come from Italy or Ireland or Germany were as American as he was.

Sometimes at night, when the cadets were given a free hour, he would sit on the plain overlooking the Hudson River and think of these things. He knew now that one state was no more important than another, and that it was the country as a whole that was important.

"Back home," he would think, "people are always arguing about religion or politics. Here we never argue about those things. We've learned that every man has a right to his church and to his political party. That's part of being American, so why argue about it?"

The summer passed all too quickly. When September came, Autie was tanned and stronger than ever. He hated to go back to the barracks, but by this time he was accepting West Point life as it came. He didn't rebel, no matter how hard the study or the discipline. He still hated to study when someone told him to study, but he managed to study just enough to get by.

The really bright spot during his second year at the Point (that's what the cadets always called it) were the letters and packages he received from his folks. From Monroe, Lydia would send cakes she had baked, and his sister Ann would send him cookies and doughnuts from New Rumley. He kept his letters home cheerful.

"My darling sister Ann," he wrote one day, "I would never leave West Point for any amount of money, for I would rather have a good education and no money than a fortune and be ignorant.

The only reason I am in a hurry to finish here is so that I can help my parents. Love, Autie."

But his parents wrote saying that they needed no help. Things were going well on the farm, his father wrote, although Mother wasn't feeling too well. Just keep on studying; just remember the dream he had had when he was four years old. If he remembered it often enough and if he helped the dream a little—why, someday it might come true.

7

☆　☆　☆　☆　☆　☆　☆　☆

LIFE AT
WEST POINT

The New Rumley Invincibles were always asking Emanuel Custer for news of Autie. By this time they had a meeting place of their own. New Rumley had built a firehouse, and most of the Invincibles were also members of the Volunteer Fire Brigade. They would sit around talking politics or crops, and one day a man named Lem

Whittaker directed his words to Emanuel Custer. "That son of yours has it pretty soft, Emanuel," said Lem. "Here you are working your hands off and he sits there at West Point having everything handed to him."

"It isn't that easy, Lem," said Emanuel, smiling. "You all want to know what life is like at West Point?"

They all nodded eagerly and sat down to listen. To them, West Point was another world. It was a far-off, mysterious place. Might as well talk about Tibet as West Point. That's why they were so eager to hear about it.

"Autie writes to us twice a week," Mr. Custer said proudly, "and he tells us what it's like. Now, to begin with, West Point is on a plain high over the Hudson River. It's real nice country around there, Autie says, except it's pretty mountainous.

"Every morning at dawn there's a fellow standing by a cannon. As soon as the dawn shows over the mountain he lets that cannon go. The first thing Autie and every other kid hears in the morning is a *boom* and then the drum corps starts. They've been waiting for that gun. As soon as it goes off they beat the long reveille.

"Everyone is awake now. Autie has got used to wakin' up awake. Here on the farm we wake up and lie there a while half asleep. It's nice lying in bed wakin' up gradually, the way we do. But not at West Point. You've got no time to yawn or stretch or take another catnap. You've got to wake up wide awake. You tumble out of bed, wash, comb your hair, and put on your uniform fast. You've got to be out on that parade ground before the drum corps stops drummin' and fifin'."

Emanuel Custer paused. That should give Lem Whittaker some idea of how "soft" things were at West Point!

"All four companies line up out there, and every button has to be buttoned, every shoe has to be shined," Emanuel went on. "Now, the first classmen—they're the oldest—act as sergeants. The cadets stand at parade rest and then the cadet captain gives an order and the sergeants all repeat it: 'Attention Company.' Every cadet snaps to attention, his back like a ramrod, his eyes straight ahead. Then each sergeant takes out a book. He calls the roll of his company. If a cadet is late, the sergeant makes a mark opposite his name. If he doesn't answer, he'd better have a good excuse, like pneumonia or a broken leg."

"About what time would it be now, Emanuel?" Lem Whittaker asked.

"About five in the morning, and there's always a cold wind sweeping down the Hudson and hittin' the plain," Emanuel said. "Now the roll call is finished. Then the cadet captain assigns certain jobs to certain cadets—like guard duty. Then ranks are broken and Autie and Jim Parker—this year Autie and Jim have a room by themselves—run back to their barracks. They make their beds and clean their room. At five thirty the inspection group comes around. If things aren't just so, the cadets get demerits. Now the boys settle down to study . . ."

"No breakfast yet?" Lem asked, amazed.

"Not yet. They study their mathematics and at seven the bugle blows and they tumble out to form their companies again. Then they march into the mess hall for breakfast. At eight o'clock the bugle blows again. Now they march to their classes and for five hours they listen to officers trying to teach them. Five long hours in the classroom and then lunch."

"They ought to be hungry by that time," Lem remarked with a chuckle.

"Autie says they're always hungry. They have their meal at one o'clock and then go back to the classroom until four. At four they hurry to the parade ground for drill. Winter, spring, snow, rain—it doesn't matter. They drill every afternoon. They drill in platoons and then at sunset they have the dress parade of the whole battalion. The band is out for this one, and people come all the way from New York to see the dress parade. That lasts about an hour, but Autie says they like it. He also says they can march better than any other troops in the world."

"Better than the New Rumley Invincibles?" Lem Whittaker cackled.

"I don't think they could march through the woods better than we could, Lem," Emanuel said, "but I guess they are the best up there on that parade ground. When they've finished they all stand at attention, and then there is the boom of the evening gun. Before it has died away the bugler sounds 'retreat,' and the flag on top of the tall pole flutters down. Then the cadets march into the mess hall for their big meal of the day. They've got nothing to do now for an hour and a half."

"You mean they're not finished yet?" Lem asked, surprised.

"Not quite. After they're through eating they sit around the recreational hall and then that darn bugle blows again. This time it's 'To Quarters,' and they all hurry back to the barracks. They have to stay in their rooms studying until nine thirty. Mind you, every few days officers are sent around to see that the cadets really do study. If they're found reading anything except a textbook or talking—bang—another demerit on their records.

"At nine thirty the bugle sounds again. That's the signal to stop studying, to pull the covers back from their cots (they have cots in their second year), and get ready for bed. At ten o'clock, taps sounds and every light has to go out. Autie says that's all right, too, because by ten o'clock you're so darn tired you just want to collapse into bed."

"Autie have any trouble sleepin'?" Lem asked.

"Autie never had any trouble sleepin'," Mr. Custer answered. "Well, boys, that's life at West Point. You start at dawn and keep going to ten o'clock at night. You think it's a soft life, Lem?"

"Guess not, Emanuel," said Lem, and he shook his head. "When a boy finishes five years there, he's all set to be an officer in any man's army."

"Autie says they have a lot of special studies that they don't do every day. Like fencing. They really learn how to handle a sword either on foot or on horseback. And they keep physically fit. They wrestle and run, and Autie tells me," Emanuel said proudly, "that he's the best wrestler up there. And you know he always could ride a horse."

Emanuel's report on life at West Point was a good one. Autie had to work hard, but he and Jim Parker managed to have fun, too. Usually they had Sunday afternoons to themselves. One day they sat on the shore looking across the Hudson. It was a warm afternoon and the water looked inviting.

"I wonder if we could swim across that river," Autie said idly.

"I come from Missouri, Autie," Jim drawled, "and I've swum across the Mississippi River lots of times."

"Biggest river I ever swam across was the old Raisin River at Monroe," Autie said. Then he added, "What do you say we try it?"

Jim Parker grinned and started taking off his clothes. The boys stripped to their shorts and then Autie said, "Some fresh upperclassmen might see our clothes here and swipe them."

"Just like them," Jim grumbled. "Look, Autie, let's tie them together with our belts, then hitch them onto our backs and ferry them across."

Autie laughed. "Sure. Then if we meet anybody on the other side, we can get dressed."

They waded into the Hudson. It was easy until they hit the middle of the river. There was a real current there, but they were both strong swimmers and they kept right on. They finally reached the other shore. Exhausted by the long, hard swim, they waded out of the water.

"You're just in time for dinner," they heard, and looking up they saw a smiling middle-aged man. "My wife and our three boys are fixing a grand spread over there," the man said, waving an arm inland.

"I'm sorry," Autie said as he and Jim dried themselves hastily and dressed. "We didn't mean to butt in. We're cadets, and we just thought we'd take a swim."

"Come on, boys," the man urged. "We have more than enough food, and my sons have always wanted to talk to a cadet."

Autie and Jim went with him. Soon they saw a campfire around which a woman and three small boys were seated. When the cadets got close to the fire their eyes popped out at the food they saw. There were steaks and corn-on-the-cob and homemade cake.

One of the small boys looked up at Jim and asked solemnly, "Are you a general?"

"Me? Not me." Jim Parker laughed. "But my friend here, Autie Custer, will be a general someday. You just wait and see."

Autie looked up, startled. Well as he knew Jim, he had never mentioned his life's ambition. How had Jim known it?

"Where did you ever get that idea, Jim?" Autie asked, trying to sound casual.

To his surprise, Jim looked serious. "I've just got a feeling, Autie. Just a feeling. You'll either bust out of West Point or you'll be a famous general."

"Even famous generals have to eat," their hostess said. "Now, that steak is just about done. And this corn is all ready."

One of her sons said to Autie, "I hear you have to study very hard to be a cadet. Is it hard at West Point? What is it really like there?"

Autie looked down at the sizzling steak on his plate and he thought of the warm friendship between Jim and him. He felt, too, the friendliness of these nice people. He looked up and said, "How is life at West Point? I can tell you in one word, sonny—wonderful. That's all. It's just wonderful!"

8

☆ ☆ ☆ ☆ ☆ ☆ ☆ ☆

AUTIE MAKES
A MISTAKE

Suddenly every lesson, every drill, every bit of target practice had a new meaning for the cadets. The date was December 10, 1860. The South was threatening to secede from the Union. That would mean war—real war, with brother fighting brother.

Cadet Paul Young was a good friend of Autie's.

Paul was from Georgia, but Autie never thought of him as having thoughts that were different from his own. One day after supper Autie found himself sitting next to Paul in the recreation hall.

"What's going to happen, Paul?" he asked.

"What's going to happen?" Paul's voice was grave. "War is going to happen. I've known it for a year. I can tell from the letters I get from home. Yes, Autie, there's going to be war, and because I'm from Georgia, I'm going to go home and ask Governor Brown to give me a cavalry regiment. You? You'll get a cavalry regiment too—you're the best rider here at the Point. And one day, Autie, you and I may be fighting against each other."

"I hate to think of that," Autie said miserably. "I never thought I'd ever fight anything but Indians."

"First we have to settle this argument between the states," Paul said. "When you believe in something, you sometimes have to fight for it."

"I'm confused," Autie said, honestly puzzled. "I've always felt that a state was merely part of the country as a whole—that it had no life except what it received from the Federal Government. Now the southern states are actually saying they're equal to or superior to the Federal Government."

"It's hard to understand, Autie," Paul said sadly, "unless you've been brought up in the South. We believe we have certain rights that no Federal Government can take away from us. We're as honest in our belief as, well—say—you are in yours. But anyhow, nothing's going to happen right away."

It did happen soon enough, though. On December 20, 1860, South Carolina seceded from the Union, and Mississippi, Alabama, Florida, Georgia, Louisiana, and Texas soon followed.

One by one the cadets from southern states resigned from West Point to go home. Cadets Young, Kelley, and Ball were three of Autie's classmates who left. It was a sad farewell, for there was no ill feeling against the southerners. They were doing their duty as they saw it.

And then, on April 12, 1861, Fort Sumter was fired upon. This was an act of war, and the whole nation became inflamed. At that time Winfield Scott was general in chief of the army. He needed officers badly, so he immediately ordered that the five-year West Point course be reduced to four years. This meant that Autie's class would graduate in June.

Autie knew now that he would actually be fighting within a few months. Books? He forgot about them. He spent all of his spare time at the riding academy, hardening his body. He spent hours at the rifle range, and with the fencing instructor. Discipline, so far as the classroom went, was not as strict. These boys would have to fight soon, and the instructors knew that was all they thought about. But there were final examinations in June.

In the beginning there had been 125 plebes in Autie's class. That number had dwindled to 34. When the examinations were finished, Autie found that he was 34th in his class of 34. But even the officers didn't care. They laughed and told Autie he'd still make a good officer. It was really only during the last few months that he had neglected his books. The officers who taught the cadets realized that it was impossible for a high-spirited lad like Autie to keep his mind on studying with the country up in arms.

Examinations were over, but graduation was still to come. It was now that Autie did something that almost ended his whole military career. One afternoon he was officer of the guard, which meant he was responsible for keeping order among the other cadets. Two plebes were having an argument, and they decided to settle it with their fists. They started to fight, and some of their classmates grabbed them and held them.

Autie had seen the whole thing. He walked up and said, "Why not let them fight it out fairly and squarely? Stand back, the rest of you."

They did, and the two boys started in. Just then two officers, Lieutenants Hazen and Merrill, appeared on the scene. They stopped the fight and looked sternly at Cadet Autie Custer.

"You are officer of the guard today," Lieutenant Hazen said sternly. "Why didn't you stop this riot?"

"Riot?" Autie repeated. "It was just a private fight."

"Report yourself under arrest, Cadet Custer," Lieutenant Hazen said. "Under the rules, which you should have known, a fight in public like this is a 'riot.' "

"Yes, sir," Autie said, saluting with serious face.

Five minutes later he was in the guardhouse, and Colonel John F. Reynolds, commandant of West Point, was interviewing the two lieutenants who had merely done their duty in reporting Autie. They liked him, but duty, not likes or dislikes, comes first in the army.

Colonel Reynolds had to report the affair to his superiors in Washington, and they ordered a court-martial. If Autie was found guilty, he would be dismissed in disgrace and all of his hard work would be for nothing. His dream would be ended.

As Autie waited for the trial, new orders came from Washington. His class was to be commissioned immediately and sent to Washington. The fighting had begun in earnest. Some called it the Civil War. Others called it the War Between the States. The whole cadet corps was excited by the news, but Autie sat in the guardhouse, completely heartbroken. Yet he knew in his heart that he was guilty. He should have stopped the fight immediately and reported the two boys. They would have received a few demerits, shaken hands, and the whole thing would have been forgotten.

The saddest day of all came when his thirty-three classmates lined up to march to the railroad station, where a train waited to take them to Washington. He heard them singing their favorite West Point song, "Benny Haven," as they marched off gaily. Autie sat there in the guardhouse. He clenched his strong hands, but he didn't feel strong. He felt like a little boy, and the tears streamed down his face.

He had let his father down. In one thoughtless moment he had thrown his whole future away.

Just then an officer came in and said kindly enough, "The court-martial is ready, Cadet Custer."

He stood erect and followed the officer. Four strange officers sat at the court-martial. The Army does not allow West Point instructors to sit as judges. They might have a grudge against the man on trial. Lieutenant Charles Benet was in charge of the court-martial. He asked Autie if he was guilty.

"Guilty, sir," Autie said, his head high.

The evidence was all against him. There wasn't a word that he or anyone else could say in his defense. When the hearing was over, Lieutenant Benet said, "The court will retire to consider its verdict. The accused will remain in custody."

Autie went back to the guardhouse. The day passed slowly. So did the next day, but there was no word from the court. Autie couldn't sleep, couldn't eat. How could he ever face his father again? How could he face his mother and his sisters Lydia and Ann?

On the third morning there was a rap at his door. It opened. There stood a stern-looking officer Autie had never seen before. Autie leaped to his feet and stood at attention.

"Yes, sir?" he said.

"I have orders from Washington for you," the officer said, handing over an official-looking document.

Autie's hands trembled as he took the envelope and opened it. His whole future, his whole life, would be decided by what was in that envelope.

9

☆ ☆ ☆ ☆ ☆ ☆ ☆ ☆

A HORSE NAMED WELLINGTON

Autie was astounded at what he read. He just couldn't believe it! This was his commission as second lieutenant in the United States Army, and with it were orders to report to the adjutant general in Washington at once for assignment.

"But . . . but what about the court-martial,

sir?" he asked the officer who had brought the letter.

"Don't worry about it." The officer smiled. "The army needs officers badly. I guess you have good friends in Washington—perhaps some of your classmates, or perhaps some of the officers here at the Point. But anyhow, forget the court-martial."

"When shall I leave for Washington?" Autie asked, still scarcely able to believe what he had heard.

"It says 'immediately,' " the officer said dryly. "In the army, 'immediately' means 'right away.' "

Twenty-four hours later, Lieutenant George Armstrong Custer was in Washington. He went looking for his classmates and someone told him their headquarters was at a hotel called the Ebbit House. He hurried there and found that the only classmate who still remained in the city was his old roommate, Jim Parker. The rest had left for the front. Jim was in one of the hotel rooms.

He leaped up and threw his arms around Autie. Autie told him all about the court-martial and what had happened.

"But it's all over," he said happily. "Now, Jim, you and I will be out fighting those rebels together."

He stopped when he saw Jim Parker's face. It was white, and his eyes were sad.

"You forget that my home is in Missouri," Jim said sadly.

"Isn't Missouri what they call a border state?"

Jim nodded. "Yes, it's kind of divided. Some are for the Union. Others are for the Confederacy. My family is all for the South, and you have to stick with your family, Autie."

Autie sat down, saddened, and read an official-looking paper that Jim handed him. It was from the War Department, and it said that Second Lieutenant James Parker had been dismissed from the service.

"I tried to resign, Autie," Jim said with tears in his eyes. "They wouldn't let me resign; they dismissed me. I'm off tomorrow to join Jeff Davis."

"This isn't my idea of war," Autie said, "where friends like us fight each other."

"Nothing we can do about it," Jim said. "But if ever I capture you, I'll take good care of you."

"That goes for me, too," Autie said, shaking hands with his old friend. Then he left to find out what the war news was. From the Union viewpoint it wasn't very good. General Beauregard's Confederate forces had pushed the Union Army under General McDowell back to Centreville, in Virginia.

At once Autie hurried to the office of the adjutant general. He had to wait until two in the morning to see him. But the wait was worth it.

When the young lieutenant was finally admitted to the office, he found a tall, dignified-looking man with the adjutant general. This was the great General Winfield Scott, hero of the Mexican War, head of the whole Union Army. He shook hands with Autie, smiling a little at the golden-haired second lieutenant.

"A great many of you young West Pointers are here in Washington drilling volunteers," the general said. "Would you like to be assigned to that duty?"

Autie's face fell, but he managed to say, "I'll gladly accept any duty you assign me to, sir."

Scott looked at him thoughtfully. "Have you had much experience at riding?"

"I was practically born on a horse, sir," Autie said earnestly, and that was true enough.

"I have some dispatches I want sent to General McDowell in the field," General Scott said. "You are not afraid of a night ride?"

"I was brought up in the wilderness, sir," Autie said eagerly. "I can ride any horse any time."

This wasn't just boasting; it was the truth.

"Report back in two hours, Lieutenant Custer," said General Scott with a smile. "I'll have the dispatches ready."

Autie walked in a state of excitement. But suddenly he realized that he didn't have a horse. In the outer office there was a captain who was General Scott's aide. Autie told him of the assignment General Scott had given him. Where, he asked, could he find a horse?

"Son, I don't believe there's a mount left in Washington," the captain said sadly. "They're all up with McDowell."

An hour later Autie found out that this was just about true. Then, by sheer luck, he saw a soldier riding a horse and leading another one by its bridle. Autie recognized the trooper as a man who had been a riding teacher at West Point. The trooper shook hands warmly with the young lieutenant, whom he had taught for so long.

"Where are you leading that horse?" Autie asked.

"I've been stationed at the front with General McDowell," the trooper said. "I was sent back here by Colonel Griffin of his staff to pick up this extra horse and lead him back."

Autie blurted out his story of having a wonderful assignment and of not being able to find a horse.

"Well, Lieutenant," and the trooper smiled, "if you rode this horse, he'd get to Colonel Griffin a lot quicker than if I led him. And it's a horse you've ridden before."

Autie looked closely at the big horse. "It's Wellington!" he cried happily. Wellington was a horse which only the best horsemen at West Point were permitted to ride. At mention of his name the horse perked up his ears and whinnied.

"He knows me," Autie pointed out.

"Just see that the mount gets safely to Colonel Griffin." The trooper smiled again. "You'll find him with General McDowell."

Now that Autie had his mount (the cavalry term for a horse), he hurried back to headquarters and found the dispatches ready for him. He was told how to reach Centreville, where General McDowell was, and then he set out through the night. He had been given no instructions as to what he was to do after delivering the dispatches. He assumed, therefore, that he was to make himself useful to McDowell in whatever way he could. The army wasn't too well organized in those days.

Wellington loped along without effort. In the distance Autie saw the flickering lights of campfires, and his heart quickened. He pressed his knees against Wellington's flanks (you didn't even have to use your spurs on this great horse) and Wellington lengthened his stride. At last Autie drew rein in front of the biggest tent in the encampment, rightly guessing this would be General McDowell's headquarters.

To his amazement he saw a familiar figure outside the tent. It was Lieutenant Joshua Kingsbury, the general's aide-de-camp. Kingsbury had graduated from West Point only a year before.

"I have dispatches from General Scott for General McDowell," Autie said, slipping down from his mount.

"He'll be glad to get them. Just wait a minute," Kingsbury said. He took the dispatches into the tent and came out a moment later.

"Now that's done with, Autie, let's get this mount fed and stabled," he suggested. "Then we'll have some breakfast."

"The mount belongs to Colonel Griffin," Autie said. Wellington was taken in charge by a trooper and then the two hungry young officers sat down to a breakfast of Virginia ham, eggs, and corn muffins.

"Now tell me the news," Autie demanded.

"You left West Point just three days ago, didn't you, Autie?" Kingsbury asked.

Autie nodded.

"And tomorrow you're going to be shot at."
The aide smiled.

"Shot at?" Autie was puzzled.

"We attack Beauregard tomorrow," Kingsbury said casually. "And as long as you're here, you may as well join the party."

"Wonderful," Autie said eagerly. "Where will the battle take place?"

"At Bull Run," Kingsbury said.

"I've never heard of Bull Run," Autie told him.

10

☆ ☆ ☆ ☆ ☆ ☆ ☆ ☆

AUTIE IS SHOT AT

Bull Run was only a quiet little stream in Virginia, but it became the most famous stream in North America during the next three days.

Lieutenant Custer was assigned to Company G, Second Cavalry. A young bugler in the company, Joseph Fought, quickly attached himself to the new young lieutenant. He was right at Autie's side when the company made its first charge. They rode pell-mell up a hill to support an infantry company that was in bad trouble.

Autie never had to think about riding. He rode a horse instinctively, the way a cowboy rides a horse. But dashing up that hill at the head of his company, with bullets whistling around his ears, he had a lot of other things to think about.

All young soldiers wonder whether they'll be afraid the first time they're shot at. To Autie's surprise, he wasn't afraid—merely angry. He knew now how well he and the other cadets had been trained at West Point. No, he wasn't afraid, but bugler Joseph Fought was afraid. He was afraid that Autie Custer would be killed. Autie's cavalry hat had blown off and his bright golden hair made him stand out. And Autie was in the lead, out front where the bullets were thickest.

Autie did have one moment of panic. "Should I use my gun or my saber?" he kept asking himself. Not being sure, he held his pistol in his right hand and his sword in his left. Dropping the reins, he guided his mount with his knees. And so Autie Custer led his first charge with "no hands."

It was successful. The infantry company was saved, but soon the Confederate artillery found the range and Joseph Fought had to blow retreat on his bugle. Retreat? That's all the Union Army did during the next two days. In two days Autie learned as much as he had learned during his four years at West Point.

The biggest lesson he learned was that the Confederate Army could fight just as well as the Union Army—and maybe better. Of course, it too was led by West Point graduates.

The Union Army's retreat toward Washington became a rout, but Autie Custer's company was the last to leave the battlefield. He and his men protected the retreating infantry, retreating themselves only when the Confederate artillery started to splash shells around them.

They retreated past Centreville, and then the rain began. By now, General McDowell had ordered the whole army to return to Arlington, outside of Washington, where there were forts and trenches and breastworks. They would be safe there. That is, if they could get most of their artillery back with them.

At a bridge outside of Centreville, a dozen guns were bogged down in the mud. These had to be saved. Men were trying to lash the tired horses into pulling out of the mud the big wheels on which the guns were mounted. The men had to be protected while they worked.

Company G was assigned to "cover" the artillery. Custer led three charges against the advancing Confederate infantry. He didn't know it then, but he was attacking troops led by the famous Stonewall Jackson. By this time, Autie realized that his pistol was more valuable than his saber. (They always called a sword a saber in the cavalry.) After all, a pistol had six shots in it, and the noise might at least scare the enemy troops.

Company G had begun the fighting with three officers. Autie, of course, was the youngest and least experienced. But in the confusion of the rain and the darkness the other two officers had disappeared or been lost or dismounted. As a result Autie Custer, five days out of West Point, found himself in charge of a company.

Three times he led his men. Three times they were driven back, but this gave the Union forces time to pull the heavy guns over the bridge and to start them on the road toward Washington. At that point a courier came to Custer and told him to sound retreat. Young Joseph Fought had his bugle to his lips before the order was out. He was very young but very smart, too, and he knew that if Company G didn't get out of there, they would be outflanked and captured.

So Custer led the company back across the bridge toward Arlington. Finally, the very last company to retreat, they reached the camp. Custer found tents for his troops and made sure that the tired horses were fed and stabled.

Autie was reeling with tiredness. Young Joseph Fought went up to him.

"Horses and men are taken care of, Lieutenant," he said.

"I'd better make sure," Autie mumbled.

"I've made sure, sir," Joseph said. "You haven't eaten in two days. You haven't slept in three. You must get out of this rain or you'll be sick."

"I've slept out in the rain before," Autie said. "The ground under this tree looks soft to me. I'll take a little nap right here."

With that he slid to the ground, stretched out, yawned once, and was fast asleep. He didn't know it, of course, but while he slept they were talking about him around the campfires. "Who was that young officer with the golden hair?" some trooper would ask, and another would say, "Autie Custer—just out of West Point."

The talk was not confined to the enlisted men. Senior officers were saying, "Keep your eye on young Custer. He saved our artillery at the bridge outside Centreville." The talk reached the top staff officers, and even while Autie Custer slept, his name was put on the list of those "cited for bravery." There weren't many cited for bravery during the first Battle of Bull Run.

Autie slept for twenty hours. When he awoke there was Joseph Fought with hot coffee for him, and the Washington newspaper. As he handed the paper to Autie, his eyes shone. The news of the tragic defeat (from the Union side) was there, but another story told of those cited for bravery, and among them was the name of Second Lieutenant George Armstrong Custer.

"You're a hero, Lieutenant," Joseph said happily. "Everyone is talking about it."

"I didn't do anything," Autie said.

"Maybe the generals and the staff officers know better." Joseph chuckled.

"I'll mail this to my father," Autie said, trying to keep the pride out of his voice. "And I must go and see Congressman Bingham."

That afternoon, after he had washed and changed his uniform, he obtained permission to visit the Capitol. When he reached it he found that each congressman had an office of his own. He finally found Congressman Bingham's office. He knocked at the door and a voice called out, "Come in." He entered. There was Congressman Bingham.

"Sir, you won't remember me," Autie began,

"but I've been in my first battle. I tried to do my best. I felt I ought to report to you because it was through you I got my appointment to West Point."

"Not know you, son?" The big congressman roared with laughter. "I've been reading about you and hearing about you all day. You're my boy, Autie Custer!"

And he put his arms around the shoulders of the boy who had made good.

"Your father will be proud of you when he gets my letter." Congressman Bingham chuckled.

11

☆ ☆ ☆ ☆ ☆ ☆ ☆ ☆

THE DREAM
COMES TRUE

Back in New Rumley, Autie Custer was suddenly a hero. Congressman Bingham did write to Emanuel Custer, and no doubt Autie's father read the letter aloud to the Invincibles.

Autie kept writing home faithfully, and one day Emanuel could report proudly that his son was now Captain George Armstrong Custer. Promotions came fast during the Civil War.

The war dragged on. Autie spent months in Washington doing staff work, which he hated, and then he was ordered back to the field. He was an excellent cavalryman, and his superior officers gave him one dangerous mission after the other. His fellow officers liked Autie, but they used to laugh when he would say, "I'll be a general before this war is over."

They laughed because Autie was only twenty-three. Everyone admitted that he had amazing courage and a complete disregard for his own life, but an officer needed more than that to become a general.

One day he returned to headquarters, tired after having led a hard cavalry charge. Lieutenant George Yates, with whom he shared a tent, greeted him with, "Hello there, General."

"Laugh all you want, George," Autie said wearily. "I'll be a general . . ."

"I'm not laughing," Yates said. "Come inside the tent."

There on Autie's cot was a long, official-looking envelope. It was addressed to Brigadier General George Armstrong Custer.

"Somebody's fooling me," Autie said to Yates.

It just didn't seem possible that he could have been "jumped" from captain to general!

"Open it and see, Autie." Yates was excited.

Autie opened the envelope. It was his commission as brigadier general. He was assigned to command the 2nd Brigade of the Third Division, which was called the Michigan Brigade.

Autie sat down on the cot. He couldn't believe it, not even when George Yates let out an excited yell and the other officers came rushing in. George told them the news. The men crowded around Autie, pressing his hand, but he could only sit there with tears in his eyes. His dream had come true. He was not only a general but he was the youngest general in the army.

His orders were to report to his new command right away. He found the Michigan Brigade camped on some ridges above a little town called Gettysburg in Pennsylvania.

A day later the most talked-about battle of the Civil War began. The Michigan Brigade made two great cavalry charges to take hills held by the Confederate artillery. Autie, of course, led the charges, his golden hair streaming in the wind. There weren't many casualties in Custer's own unit and his men began talking proudly about "Custer's Luck." They liked to follow a lucky general.

For the North, the Battle of Gettysburg marked the turning point of the Civil War. General Robert E. Lee was forced to withdraw his Confederate forces to Virginia.

In 1863 there was a lull in the fighting and Autie was given a furlough. He hurried back to New Rumley to be treated as a hero.

But while he was in New Rumley, he kept thinking about Elizabeth Bacon—the girl who had called out to him, "Hello, you Custer boy." He had often wondered what that girl was really like. He had written to her many times during the war, but her letters to him had been very formal and polite. And her father, a strict parent, had at last forbidden her to answer Autie's letters.

Autie went to Monroe to find that Elizabeth Bacon, whom everyone called Libbie, was also thinking about him, and now that Autie was a general her father was much more friendly. Soon they were married, and then Autie went back to his army post.

The Civil War was a long war, and he saw plenty of action, but finally it was all over. General Custer led his troops in the victory parade in Washington. His attractive young wife looked on proudly as Autie, who was now a major general, rode by on his big white horse. In the crowds that cheered him stood Emanuel Custer, proudly watching his son. Congressman Bingham was there too.

When the parade was over, Autie, Libbie, and Emanuel went back to Monroe. The war had come to an end and the nation was weeping over its dead. In the White House, Abe Lincoln was trying to heal the awful wounds of war; trying to bring the North and the South together again.

Autie Custer never did like to just "sit around," and that was what he was doing in Monroe. He loved being with his wife, but he was a soldier. He couldn't be happy doing a little fishing or going to Sunday night suppers with the neighbors. His father noticed how restless he was.

"Son, you ought to be the happiest man alive," he said. "So far as I know, you're the only one who ever had a dream as a child of four who made the dream come true."

"It only came half true," Autie said gloomily.

"What do you mean, son?"

"I always said I wanted to be a general and fight Indians," Autie said. "I became a general, all right, but I never did get to fight any Indians."

"Maybe you will someday." His father laughed, not really believing it.

Even while he was speaking, the Sioux, the Cheyenne, and the Arapaho tribes were uniting to fight the white man. A group of peaceful Cheyennes had been living quietly at Sand Creek, Colorado. For no reason at all the militia attacked them and killed nearly all of them. Ordinarily the Sioux and the Arapahos would be fighting against the Cheyennes. Now they began to think that if the white man could break a treaty and attack peaceful Cheyennes, why, they—the Sioux and the Arapahos—might be next on the list. So they donned their paint and went on the warpath.

Back in Monroe, Autie followed the news eagerly. He was no longer a general. In the army there are wartime ranks and peacetime ranks. A wartime general (unless he has been a general for years) is usually demoted in rank when the war is over. So Autie was now Captain Custer. But if there was any more real fighting, he would surely become a general again. And fighting was what he had been trained to do.

Finally his orders came. Autie was to go to Fort Riley, Kansas. This wasn't quite the Wild West, but it was the country of the Cheyennes, and Autie was keenly excited. Libbie insisted upon going with him. So in late October 1866, off they started for Fort Riley.

When they arrived there, they found General Hancock in command. Custer—who had been raised to the rank of lieutenant colonel—found the 7th Cavalry waiting for him. It didn't look like much of a regiment, Autie thought. Discipline was poor because the soldiers had been idle for a long time. But he knew he could make the 7th Cavalry a real fighting outfit again.

12

☆　　☆　　☆　　☆　　☆　　☆　　☆　　☆

THE INDIAN FIGHTER

In Kansas and the surrounding territories Autie Custer had to learn a new type of warfare. Indians didn't fight like West Pointers. Soldiers had to be on guard at all times. The Indians fought the way the British Commandos later fought in World War II. Small groups would attack silently, quickly, savagely, and then fade into the night.

They blew no bugles to announce their attacks. Their surefooted little ponies were as silent as they, and Custer discovered that the Indians were better horsemen than West Point had ever trained.

They were deadly shots even from galloping horses. And they were fearless. Each Indian carried a tomahawk, a hunting knife, a bow, and a quiver of arrows slung on his pack. In addition, most of them carried breech-loading rifles.

Autie learned to tell the Cheyennes from the Sioux, and the Sioux from the Arapahos. He learned to recognize the important Cheyenne chiefs: Roman Nose, Bull Bear, White Horse, Medicine Arrow, and others.

During the next few years Custer also learned the Indian way of fighting, and how best to fight them. It was hard to fight them in the summer, when they could silently slip away through the forests. The heavy woods concealed them, and if Custer's men did see them, the little Indian ponies could outrun his best cavalry.

The best time to fight Indians was in the fall or winter because they never carried food for their horses. That worked all right for them in the summer, for there was good grazing for a hundred miles in every direction. But in the winter the snow covered the grass and the Indian ponies grew thin and weak and they lost their speed. Indians could hide in the heavy summer foliage, but the forests were bare in the late fall and winter.

These were some of the things Autie Custer learned. And he made sure the 7th Cavalry learned them too.

At first they learned their lessons the hard way. Unwary sentries sleeping at their posts would be found scalped in the morning. Stragglers in the line of march would suddenly hear wild war whoops, and those would be the last sounds they would ever hear.

Although the 7th Cavalry learned to hate Indians, not all Indians were warriors. There were thousands who merely wanted to live in peace with the white man. But the 7th Cavalry had lost many soldiers, and they blamed the Indians for these losses.

In the fall of 1868 Autie received the following order from General Phil Sheridan, head of the army in the West and one of the great heroes of the Civil War:

. . . to proceed south in the direction of the Antelope Hills, thence go toward the Washita River, the supposed winter seat of the hostile tribes; to

*destroy their villages and their ponies; to kill or
hang all warriors . . .*

The 7th Cavalry was ready. It was a long march
to the Washita River, in what is now the state of
Oklahoma. (At that time it was in Indian territory.) But the nine hundred men of the Seventh
were equal to any march. Autie Custer no longer
wore his elegant blue uniform with its bright
brass buttons. He wore frontier clothes—buffalo
boots, a buffalo coat, and a broad-brimmed campaign hat. It was hard to tell him from his scouts,
California Joe and Jack Corbin, except for his long
golden hair. Nobody else had hair like that.

In late November the men set out for the
Washita River. There was a light snow under-
foot, but the Seventh marched quickly. Suddenly, galloping toward them, they saw
California Joe. He had come with a warning that
there were Indians ahead.

Autie had a group of friendly Osage Indians
with him and he ordered two of their chiefs,
Little Beaver and Hard Rope, to learn the size of
this Indian force. The pair disappeared into the
darkness and Autie waited impatiently.

When they returned they said it was a big
Cheyenne village whose chief was Black Kettle.

"We will avenge the men of the Seventh who

have been scalped!" Autie Custer cried to his men, and an answering roar came from the Seventh. Then Autie ordered the charge.

The snow which had been falling gently now began to swirl madly against the faces of the troopers. It was bitter cold, and Autie knew that the Indians would be huddled in their tepees. The Seventh made its charge. The Indians were surprised, but they always slept with their weapons by them, and for a time there was a bitter fight. Then the Indians seemed to fade away.

But Autie wasn't fooled. He knew they had retreated only to attack again.

"Where is Black Kettle?" Autie asked Hard Rope.

"Dead," the Osage said.

From the ravines and gullies beyond the village there came wild war whoops. In the burning village a weird chant began.

"What is that?" Autie asked Hard Rope.

"It is the women. They sing the death song," the Osage scout replied.

Now the Cheyennes had formed into small groups, making desperate attacks upon the village, which was being held by the 7th Cavalry. Many got through. Autie, astride his big white horse, kept swinging his saber. He seemed to lead a charmed life. His most trusted aide, Captain Louis Hamilton, was shot in the head and slipped off his horse, dead.

The night air was filled with the sharp cracks of the rifles, the cries of the wounded, and the terrifying war whoops of the Indians. Autie led his men out of the village. He gave only one order: "Hunt them down."

By this time the Indians had hidden themselves in gullies and behind the snow-covered hills. When their ammunition was gone, they used their bows and arrows. When their arrows were gone, they leaped forward with tomahawks and knives.

They were brave men, fighting for their homes, fighting for their wives and children. The odds were against them, but not one man surrendered and only the wounded were captured.

As the morning light appeared, the snow stopped and the rattle of gunfire died away. The fight was over. Autie told his bugler to recall the troops.

The bugle brought them back to the village on the gallop. Many Indians lay dead in the snow. There were few casualties among the white men. But Major Joel Elliot and nineteen men were missing. Where were they?

Several weeks later they were found two miles from the village. All were dead.

13

☆　　☆　　☆　　☆　　☆　　☆　　☆　　☆

CALIFORNIA JOE AND BIG EARS

No one knew California Joe's real name. Everyone just called him California Joe. But there were two things the old scout always kept near him—his pipe and his mule, Big Ears. He never even carried a gun, just a tomahawk and a hunting knife.

After the fight Autie wanted to talk to him, but California Joe was nowhere around.

"Have they got him, too?" Autie asked the Osage, Little Beaver.

Little Beaver grinned. "California Joe is too smart. No Indian will ever kill California Joe."

Just then they heard a shout from the troops. The sun was high now, and the morning clear. Approaching the village was a herd of three hundred ponies. There were three riders—two Indian women at the head of the herd, and California Joe, bringing up the rear. California Joe had his lariat out. He was swinging it over his head, urging the ponies on. Then he barked an order in Cheyenne and the two women reined in their ponies and the whole herd stopped. California Joe dismounted and walked up to Autie.

"Chief," he drawled (all officers were Chief to the old scout), "Chief, I brung in some prisoners. Two squaws and three hundred ponies."

"Where did you find them?" Custer asked in amazement.

"Where there is Injuns there is ponies," California Joe said. "While all this fightin' is goin' on, I went downstream a bit, and sure enough there's the ponies. No braves there, only these two squaws. So I told these two squaws to round them up. And here we are, Chief."

"Joe," Autie said, laughing, "you can have

your pick of these ponies. Which one do you want?"

"Not me, Chief." California Joe shook his head. "I'll stick to my Big Ears. Now, Chief, I got a little news for you. I talked to these squaws and learned something."

"What?" Autie asked.

"These Cheyennes of Black Kettle ain't the only Injuns around here. No siree. About five miles down the river the Comanches is winterin'. And beyond them the Kiowas and the Arapahos. And over the river the Apaches are livin'."

"You sure?" Autie asked sharply.

"No Injun ever lied to California Joe," he said. "Yes, I'm sure. And I'm sure they're gettin' set right now to march on us. I ain't no officer, but if I was, I'd be figurin' on gettin' outa here."

That was enough for Autie Custer. He knew he could rely on the word of California Joe. A lot of men thought California Joe was half Indian himself. Maybe he was. He never said. But he certainly did know a great deal about Indians.

Autie realized this. Although the young officer was brave, and sometimes reckless, he was seldom foolhardy. The 7th Cavalry was a regiment, not an army. There might be five thousand Indians out there. It was time to withdraw.

He ordered the regiment to head for Camp Supply, which was army headquarters.

Autie sent California Joe and Jack Corbin ahead to inform General Sheridan what had happened. Big Ears, the mule, wasn't fast, but he could keep on going day and night. The Seventh, with its heavy supply wagons, had to move slowly. A few hours before the Seventh reached Camp Supply in the Oklahoma territory, California Joe returned with a dispatch from General Sheridan congratulating the regiment on its achievement. The general said that he would review the Seventh as it entered camp.

It was a strange-looking procession that entered Camp Supply to pass before General Phil Sheridan. First came the Osage guides, who felt as though they had gained the victory themselves. They yelled their Osage war cries and fired off their guns.

After them came California Joe, Jack Corbin, and six other white scouts. Then came fifty Indian prisoners wrapped in their bright-colored blankets. They had been captured along with 875 ponies and 1,100 buffalo robes. They rode erect on their ponies with their heads held high. Then came the band, blasting "Garry Owen," an old West Point favorite of Autie's. Then came Autie on his white horse with his regiment behind him. In the rear were the supply wagons and the ambulances.

General Sheridan had always liked Autie Custer. He congratulated him.

"But remember," he told Autie, "this was merely the opening battle in the war against all the enemy Indian tribes south of the Arkansas River."

"We're ready to march tomorrow, sir," Autie said proudly.

"I won't ask that of you," said General Sheridan with a smile, "but have your men ready in a week."

"Yes, sir." Autie saluted smartly.

General Sheridan was determined to wipe out all the Cheyennes. This was a cruel, unjust decision. There were certainly some bad Indians, but there were many good Indians, too. The United States government had made many peace treaties with the Indians. Yet if one small band of outlaw Indians attacked a stagecoach or a settlement, the treaty was forgotten and the whole tribe condemned to death.

The Indians had lost faith in the promises of the white man, and looking back, how can anybody blame them? Now, after the killing of Black

Kettle and the burning of his village, all the tribes were up in arms. They had given this Cheyenne chief the name of Black Kettle the Peacemaker. He was not a warrior. If the white man could kill even a peacemaker, the Indians felt that the white man would kill any Indian. So in self-defense they united.

While the Seventh was at Camp Supply, word came that a group of Cheyennes had captured two white women and were holding them not far from Black Kettle's village. Sheridan gave Autie Custer an order: "Rescue those two women." The Seventh had had only four days' rest, but it was now a veteran fighting force and didn't need much rest. Again they were off on the march.

They found the village, but it was deserted and the fires were cold.

"We'll keep on until we find them," Autie decided.

On they went . . . one week . . . two weeks . . . with only short rests for weary horses and tired men. But they were close to the Cheyenne now. California Joe and the Osage scouts had no trouble following the trail.

At the end of the second week a group of troopers out looking for fresh meat surprised a party of Cheyennes around a fire. It was merely a small hunting party. Before the Indians could reach for their guns, the troopers had captured them. They were brought into camp and California Joe gave a whoop of joy.

"Big Head and Dull Knife!" he shouted. "Two of the biggest Cheyenne chiefs."

"Maybe we can use them." Custer's quick mind had already thought of a scheme to get the two captive women back unharmed.

On Monday of the third week they came across a deserted campsite. The fires were out, but the ashes were still warm. This was a sign to Custer that the Cheyennes weren't far off.

"Big band of Cheyenne," Little Beaver said. "Three hundred fifty lodges."

Autie tightened his belt, called for one piece of hardtack for every man, and then led them on. Dawn found them on a hill, and there spread below them was the Cheyenne encampment. Autie's fingers trembled as they touched his gun, but this was no time for shooting. His orders were, "Rescue those women." He knew that the captives would be killed at the sound of the first shot.

Autie ordered his men to spread out into attacking position, but not to fire. He said that he and Lieutenant William Cook, his aide, would go to the village alone and unarmed. The troopers thought he had gone crazy.

"They'll kill you if you do that," one of the officers said.

"They'll kill the two women if I don't," Autie said grimly. "Come on, Cook."

14

☆ ☆ ☆ ☆ ☆ ☆ ☆ ☆

CUSTER TO
THE RESCUE

By this time the whole Cheyenne village was
alert. Hundreds of eyes followed Autie and Cook
as they rode slowly down the slope that led into
a plain. Autie, followed by Cook, wheeled his
horse in a circle. Twice he trotted in a circle, the
Indian signal for a conference.

Then he and Cook reined in their horses. What

would it be? A volley of shots that would kill them both, or an offer to hold a meeting?

Three Indians on horseback rode slowly toward them, their bows held high in the air, a signal of a truce. But did they mean it? The white man had broken a treaty with the Cheyenne. Would the red man break a truce?

"Who is your chief?" Autie demanded when the two Indians had reached him.

"Medicine Arrow," one of the Indians said proudly. This was a famous chief, head of all the Cheyennes. Once he had been called Stone Forehead because during a fight with the Shoshones he had been hit twice on the forehead with a tomahawk, but neither blow had killed him. In addition to being a warrior he was an Indian priest and keeper of the four sacred arrows. The white man always called Indian priests medicine men, so now he was called Medicine Arrow.

"I want to talk to him," Custer said. The two Indians nodded gravely and turned their horses around. Autie and Cook followed them. They entered the village amid absolute silence; two unarmed men in the center of a thousand armed Indians.

The faces of the Indians were filled with hatred. Many had lost relatives when Custer raided Black Kettle's village. Had Custer shown the slightest sign of fear, the Indians would have sent a hundred quivering arrows into him. But his head was high and his face calm. Lieutenant Cook followed his lead.

They reached the brightly painted lodge where the chief lived. Autie and Cook dismounted. Autie stepped forward, but the two Indians barred Cook's way.

"Stay here," one of them said to Cook.

So Autie Custer walked into the lodge alone. Medicine Arrow sat in front of the fire. He motioned Custer to sit at his right. Eight other chiefs and an interpreter filed in to make a circle around the fire.

Medicine Arrow was an old man with a sad face. He had seen hundreds of his brothers killed by the white man. Now, sitting here beside him was one of those who had killed his brothers.

The old Indian chief took a long-stemmed pipe in his hand, put tobacco into it, and then reached out to the fire to scoop some glowing embers into the bowl. When the tobacco was lit, he passed the pipe to Custer.

Autie puffed on it, inwardly hoping that he wouldn't cough, for Autie had never smoked in his life. Then he passed the pipe back to Medicine Arrow. Not a word had been spoken. Medicine Arrow did not put the pipe to his lips. He passed it to the next chief, who, without smoking, passed it on again. It made the circle, but not one Indian took a puff from the pipe.

Autie felt his muscles grow tense. Had they all puffed at the pipe, it would have meant, "You are our guest. You will not be harmed." But none had smoked the pipe, so this was not a pipe of peace. Would he get out of here alive? Autie wondered. Probably not.

"I come in peace, Medicine Arrow," Autie said. "I carry neither gun nor knife."

The interpreter translated the conversation between the two.

"Why do you come?" Medicine Arrow asked.

"You have two white women here, Medicine Arrow," Autie said. "I want them."

"They are our captives," Medicine Arrow said, and the other chiefs grunted approval.

"The Cheyennes are great fighters," Custer said. "They do not make war on women. Your chiefs Big Head and Dull Knife are not as great as you, but they would never make war upon women."

"Why do you say Big Head and Dull Knife?" Medicine Arrow asked.

"Because they are my captives," Custer said calmly.

There was a startled silence. They hadn't

known that two of their most important warrior chiefs had fallen captives to Custer.

"I do not wish to hang such great warriors as Big Head and Dull Knife," Custer went on, "but the ropes are ready. Hanging is a shameful death for a Cheyenne."

No one said a word. Custer remained silent. He knew Indians. He knew now that he held a slight advantage. Medicine Arrow would feel disgraced if two of his important chiefs were hanged. To be shot or knifed was honorable; to be hanged meant that the spirit could never leave the body to find its way to the afterlife. Custer sat there before the fire, with no expression at all on his face.

"If the two women are brought to my camp by sunset," he finally said, "I will not have to hang Big Head and Dull Knife."

Medicine Arrow stood up. So did Autie Custer. From outside there was a swelling chorus of angry mutters. The Indians were impatient. They wanted Custer; they wanted to avenge Black Kettle.

"I come in peace," Autie said quietly. "I go in peace, or my men who have surrounded you will kill many brave Cheyennes this day."

"Go in peace," Medicine Arrow said, his eyes showing admiration for Autie's bravery. The chief walked to the opening of the lodge. He held up his hand and the muttering stopped.

"The white chief Yellow Hair goes in peace," he called out in Cheyenne.

Autie walked out and mounted his horse.

Cook, who had been standing there all during the meeting, hopped on his horse. Slowly the two rode out of the village. Slowly they walked their horses across the plain. Both expected an arrow in the back at any moment, but Autie understood the Indians. If he and Cook galloped away it would show fright. So they walked their horses until they were out of range and then they put them into a slow canter.

"Whew," Cook breathed, wiping his forehead with a handkerchief. "That was a close one."

Custer laughed. "We'll both have closer ones before we're much older."

As the two rode up the hill the Seventh set up a wild cheer. Now there was nothing to do but wait. So they waited.

The sun was just setting when two horses were seen coming across the plain. Autie, with the ever faithful Cook at his side, rode to meet them. On the horses were two happy, tearful women—Mrs. Morgan and Mrs. White.

"God bless you for what you did this day!"

Mrs. Morgan cried. Mrs. White was so overcome that she couldn't say a word.

"My doctors will take good care of you," Custer said. "And I have two friendly Indian women with me to tend to your wants."

"Our clothes are ruined," Mrs. Morgan said. "All torn and tattered."

"I was so sure we would get you back, ladies," Custer said, "that I took the liberty of bringing along some clothes for you. The Indian women will have everything you need."

True to his word, Autie freed the two captured Indian chiefs.

15

☆　☆　☆　☆　☆　☆　☆　☆

FIGHTING
AT THE
YELLOWSTONE

Getting those two women back was one of Autie Custer's greatest triumphs. Autie had never been a diplomat. He was a horseman, a hunter, a scout, a fighter, but nobody would ever have called him a diplomat. Still, he had shown himself to be a diplomat with old Medicine Arrow.

Custer liked to lead a charge with saber in

hand. He liked to get in close and fight. He never minded the blistering heat of the West or the long marches without water. He could drop on the ground at night and sleep like an Indian. He could go without food or, Indian fashion, swallow a mouthful of grain. But he was not tactful.

He was always getting in trouble with his superior officers. They said he was rash, reckless, and fresh. He was all of these. But he could also fight. There never was a better Indian fighter. He took big chances, but during the next few years he gave the Indians hard blows which weakened their strength.

Now there were fewer reports of stagecoaches being held up. Fewer wagon trains were being surrounded by Indians, and fewer travelers in the covered wagons were being killed.

More than once Custer was reprimanded by his superior officers in Washington. More than once he faced court-martial. But by this time he was known all over, and he and the 7th Cavalry had served in many parts of the country. He was a popular idol, and out West, ranchers and farmers breathed easier because "Yellow Hair" was feared by the Indians.

The fame of the 7th Cavalry had grown with Custer's fame. Everyone knew the Seventh. By now, Autie's young brother Tom had grown up, and he was a member of the Seventh. Tom had always been Autie's favorite, and Autie loved having Tom with him. No West Point for Tom. He was in too much of a hurry. He just enlisted and rose up through the ranks to be captain. Later young Boston Custer, whom everyone called Bos, joined the Seventh too.

If there was a tough job to be done, it was given to the Seventh. The government had decided to open the Northwest by building a railroad through it. Part of the railroad would have to go through Sioux country—territory given to the Sioux by treaty.

The Sioux, satisfied with the treaty, had been peaceful for some time. Their great chiefs, Red Cloud, Sitting Bull, and Crazy Horse, were content. But they were not content when they learned that a railroad was to be built across the Dakota and Montana territories. This, they felt, was their land. They knew that a railroad would bring forts and settlements and that their buffalo and game would disappear. They knew that it might mean death to their whole tribe.

The officials in Washington tried to reason with the chiefs. The railroad would mean progress, said the officials. The Indians replied that they didn't want progress—not the white man's progress. But the Indians were overruled, and surveyors prepared to go out to survey the land where the railroad was to be built. The government made hundreds of promises to the Indians and broke almost all of them.

Everyone has to judge for himself who was right. Was it the Indians, to whom this land had been given and who had lived in America for many generations before the white men came from Europe? Was it the Americans, who insisted that the country had to expand westward, and that they needed a railroad to help the country grow? There were good arguments on both sides, but Autie Custer didn't care about arguments. He was a soldier.

In 1873 he was ordered to go out with the surveyors, protect them, and drive hostile Indians away. Well-trained soldiers obey orders. Everything was quiet until the Seventh reached the Yellowstone River Valley. It was there that Bloody Knife, one of Autie's fine Indian scouts, became uneasy. Bloody Knife said he thought there were hostile Sioux ahead.

Custer decided to go out himself to scout the land. He took his brother Tom with him and twenty other troopers, leaving the main body in command of Captain Myles Moylan. The small party forded the river and climbed to the bluffs over the river. Autie couldn't see any Indians, but a midday haze hung over the country, making it hard to see very far.

"We'll wait until this mist clears," he said. "Meanwhile, five of you act as pickets. The rest of us will grab a little rest."

Autie lay down and promptly fell asleep. So did Tom and the others, with the exception of five who spread out to act as sentries.

Suddenly Autie was awakened by a cry of "Indians!" With one motion he grabbed his gun and leaped to his feet.

"To horse!" he cried, and every man scrambled for his horse. The Indians rode toward them, yelling as they always did, but they veered away just before they reached Autie and his men. They rode about half a mile away and then stopped. There were only about twenty of them.

"Let's go after 'em, Autie!" Tom yelled.

"Not so fast, Tom," Autie said. "It looks as if they want us to go after them. The chances are that there's a bigger force waiting somewhere to ambush us. I'll go after them alone. You stay here. I may draw their main force out of cover and then you can come a-running."

"Autie," Tom cried in alarm, "you can't go alone!"

"Dandy can outrun any Indian pony that ever lived," said Autie with a smile, and he wasn't far from the truth. Dandy was a new horse Autie had found, a big brown horse.

Autie waved and was off. He galloped pell-mell toward the Indians, and they began to run away. But he noticed that they were only trotting and not galloping. They were trying to draw him on. Well, he was willing enough. He had to find out where the main Indian force was hidden.

Then out of the corner of his right eye he saw a cloud of dust. There they were, less than half a mile away, at least three hundred of them. Autie wheeled his horse and headed back for Tom and the troopers. It looked as though the Indians had recognized him, because they were trying to cut him off from the body of troopers.

"Come on, Dandy!" he yelled, and the big horse lowered his belly and streaked. When Autie reached the bluff where his men were, he was only a quarter of a mile ahead of the Indians.

"Off your horses," Autie panted as he slid down from Dandy's neck. This was a maneuver Autie had learned long ago. If you were badly outnumbered, you could fight best from the ground.

Captain Tom and the troopers leaped down from their horses. Five of the troopers each grabbed the reins of four horses and hung on to them. That meant that five troopers now held the twenty horses.

The rest of the men, including Autie, were kneeling, taking deliberate aim at the advancing Indians. All this took about three seconds. The men were well drilled.

"Now!" Autie yelled, and the rifles crackled. The leading Indians fell and others tumbled over their fallen horses. The troopers kept firing as fast as their trigger fingers could move, pausing only to reload their weapons. The Indians plunged right on. But the firing was so fierce that they wheeled to regroup for another attack.

Autie looked at his men. He felt a fierce pride. Not one of them looked scared. They were just waiting for orders. They had the river at their backs. They couldn't retreat. They could only stay and fight it out.

"Where's Bloody Knife?" Autie cried suddenly, noticing that his favorite Indian scout was missing.

"Soon as I saw that band of Indians come out of cover," Tom drawled, "I figured we might need some help. I sent Bloody Knife back for Myles Moylan."

"That was smart of you, Captain," Autie said gravely.

"Thank you, sir," Tom said, his heart warming with pride. It wasn't often Autie praised anyone, least of all his brother.

There were heavy boulders strewn here on top of the bluff. Autie gave quick, terse orders. Two men were to get behind each boulder. Four troopers were to lead the horses back toward the river, out of the line of fire.

"We could stand them off all day in this spot," Tom said.

"We may have to." Autie laughed.

Twice more the Indians came charging. Twice more the rifles barked, leaving dead Indians all over the plain. But now ammunition was running low, and the Indians were getting ready for another assault.

"Get your knives out, men," Autie said calmly. "When your ammunition is gone, that's all we have left to fight with."

Grimly the men took knives from sheaths. And then the Indians came on. Their yells were louder than ever, but there was another sound, the sound of a bugle. It was the signal that Moylan had arrived. He was just across the river. Now he and the Seventh were dashing madly through the river. The Indians? They took one look at the onrushing Seventh and ran.

Autie put his arm around Tom's shoulders. He had good reason to be grateful to him.

16

☆　☆　☆　☆　☆　☆　☆　☆

THE 7th CAVALRY RETREATS

General D. S. Stanley was in command of the whole expedition charged with protecting the men who were surveying the railroad. When Autie and the Seventh finally joined the main body of the expedition, General Stanley gave Custer a lecture.

"Glad you're back alive, Custer," he said. "And I hope this taught you a lesson. You had no right to risk your own life by riding out alone to draw out the Indian band. You know Indians well enough to know they had a big force hidden somewhere; too big a force for your twenty troopers to handle."

"I knew Moylan wasn't far off with the Seventh," Autie said.

"If your brother Tom hadn't had sense enough to send Bloody Knife to Moylan, you'd all be dead now," General Stanley said grimly. "You're a great fighter, Custer. You have real courage. It's only your judgment I criticize. You are too reckless, and someday this disregard of the enemy may cost you your life."

"Sorry, sir, I'll try to be more careful," Autie replied. But Autie Custer just didn't know how to be careful when it came to fighting. Every other officer in the army had great respect for Sioux leaders like Sitting Bull and Crazy Horse. Autie Custer laughed at them.

"The Seventh could lick the whole Sioux tribe," he used to say.

A few days later the Seventh was ordered to return to the bluff where the fighting had taken place and to hold it against any Indian attacks.

There were no Indians in sight this time. For three days the men of the Seventh kept guard. Finally Custer grew restless.

"Where do you think those Sioux are?" he asked Bloody Knife.

"Upriver . . . eight, maybe ten miles," the scout replied.

"Well, we may as well take a look and see," Autie said. He craved action. So he ordered the Seventh to ford the river again, and they marched up the north bank. Bloody Knife had been right. About ten miles upriver they saw smoke from Indian campfires on the south bank of the Yellowstone.

"Come on, boys!" Autie cried. "Let's get them."

"River deep here," Bloody Knife protested. "River has big current."

But Autie hadn't heard. He was already in the swirling waters of the Yellowstone. So were his men. Bullets splattered around them but they kept on going. The current in the middle of the stream was so strong that the horses were turned downstream and back to shore. The Indians kept on shooting. They were hidden behind trees and boulders on the south bank.

Custer regrouped the Seventh on the north

bank, and now a really strange battle began, a battle with a river as no man's land.

Suddenly Custer heard shots from far downstream. A moment later shots came from far upstream.

"Tom, they're trying to outflank us," Autie said in worried tones. "I never knew Indians to fight like this."

"Sitting Bull and Crazy Horse have taught the Sioux to fight like the white man," Bloody Knife said.

"If we sit here we'll be surrounded," Autie said. "We'd better get going."

The bugler was told to sound "retreat," a call he had seldom played. The Seventh wasn't used to retreating. But this time retreat was the only sensible decision. So the Seventh retreated. The Indians sent a few parting volleys after them but did not pursue. Autie had lost eight men, and several others had been wounded. He knew in his heart that he should never have gone upstream looking for the Sioux. His orders had been to go to the bluffs and hold it against any Indian attackers.

The Sioux retreated from the Yellowstone, and the surveyors finished their job. The Seventh was sent to the Black Hills of the Dakota Territory.

General Sheridan had become very interested in the area. By the treaty of 1868, nearly forty-three thousand square miles had been set aside as a reservation for the Sioux Indians. Few white men had ever tried to go to the reservation, but there were many rumors about the rich supplies of game, lumber, valuable ores, and even gold to be found there.

Sheridan was even more concerned, however, about reports that the Sioux were becoming warlike again. He worried that the mysterious Black Hills would offer them a safe place to gather and hatch war plans. On June 8, 1874, General Alfred Terry, commander of the department of Dakota, sent orders to Custer to gather a force of men to explore the Black Hills and make maps of the area. They were also to look for precious ores and lumber supplies. If fighting did break out, it would be a good idea to know as much as possible about the Black Hills reservation. The army might even have to build forts there.

The expedition left Fort Lincoln a month later. They numbered about a thousand men, including soldiers, guides, interpreters, scientists, and wagon drivers. And they took with them 110 wagons and ambulances. During the day the soldiers could see smoke rising from the Sioux campfires, but the Indians always kept a day's distance from them. These were their hills, and they could hide easily here. Instead of fighting Indians, Custer and his men spent their time exploring, making maps, and looking for game, valuable ores, and lumber supplies. It was a good time for Custer. His favorites were all with him—Tom, his kid brother, Bos, and now his young nephew, Armstrong Reed, whom he had nicknamed Autie so many years ago in Monroe, had joined him.

The rumors about gold also proved to be true. Quickly news of the gold strike traveled back East, where people read about it in the newspapers. Right away miners began rushing westward to the Sioux reservation to hunt for gold. Although this gold strike never amounted to as much as the famous California Gold Rush, the new migration of white people was just one more cause for alarm among the Sioux. Again their treaty rights were being disregarded. Already a small city was growing up in what is now Custer, South Dakota.

Custer and his party returned to Fort Lincoln after spending two months in the Black Hills, but rumors of war continued. Sitting Bull and Crazy Horse were gathering all of the hostile tribes under their banners. The Cheyennes under Two Moons had joined them in their Montana hunting grounds. The tribes had been ordered to return to their reservations by January 31, 1876, or face military action. They ignored the order.

"We have been running up and down this country, but they follow us from one place to another," said Sitting Bull. The Indians were tired of broken promises. From now on they would sign no more treaties. They would fight to the death if their territory was ever again invaded by the white man.

The army decided to end the Indian threat once and for all. The 7th Cavalry was to be part of a major campaign to drive the Indians back to their reservations for good. The order came directly from President Ulysses S. Grant.

The expedition would be in the charge of General Terry, a kindly man who was cautious where Autie was reckless.

"Why not send my Seventh alone?" Autie suggested. "We can lick the whole bunch of them."

"This isn't a job for just one regiment," General Terry pointed out. "This is the big attack that will break the power of Sitting Bull and Crazy Horse forever. . . ."

"Two Indian chiefs!" said Autie with contempt.

"Autie," General Terry said quietly, "Sitting Bull is a statesman. He is a fine, sincere man. He is the leader of his people, and they worship him. Crazy Horse is as fine a cavalryman as there is in the West, and he is a brilliant military man. That is what we are up against."

"Where are the Sioux?" Autie asked.

"In the country you know well," General Terry said, walking over to the map that hung on his wall. He pointed at the Yellowstone River in the southern part of Montana.

"There are several smaller rivers flowing into the Yellowstone," he said. "There's the Powder; there's O'Fallon's Creek; there's the Tongue; and there's the Bighorn River. The Little Bighorn flows from the Bighorn to the Rosebud. Now, between these rivers are the Wolf Mountains. That's where the Sioux are now. That's where we have to go to get them."

"Yes, I know that country," Autie Custer said, looking at the map. "I've fought on the Yellowstone and along the banks of the Rosebud. I have never been around the Little Bighorn, though."

17

☆ ☆ ☆ ☆ ☆ ☆ ☆ ☆

ON TO GLORY

The goal of the army's expedition was to open up the Northwest so that a covered wagon, a stagecoach, or a group of prospectors could go through the Montana and Dakota territories without fear of attack by the resentful Indians, who had been pushed off the lands promised to them by treaty. Three separate army forces were to join in the attack.

General George Crook was coming north from Wyoming with about thirteen hundred men, including ten companies of the 3rd Cavalry. Colonel John Gibbon was moving east from Montana with four companies of the 2nd Cavalry and six companies of the 7th Infantry. General Terry was moving west from Dakota with twelve companies of the 7th Cavalry under Custer, as well as some additional troops.

At dawn on May 17, 1876, the 7th Cavalry headed westward from Fort Abraham Lincoln. At last they were marching toward battle. When Custer appeared in his buckskins, his buffalo boots, and his broad-brimmed campaign hat, a roar went up from his troops. Now they knew that there was going to be some action. Autie was mounted on his brown horse, Dandy, while his second horse, Vic, stayed at the rear with the spare horses.

By mid-June the Seventh had reached the Yellowstone River. Now they were in Indian territory and the men were quiet. The scouts always rode out far ahead of the regiment to spot any ambush.

But there was not a sign of an Indian where there should have been plenty of Indians. Custer sent Major Marcus Reno off with six companies of men to scout the land on either side of the Tongue and Powder rivers.

Meanwhile, on June 17, a combined force of Sioux and Cheyennes attacked General Crook and his cavalry forces on the upper end of the Rosebud Creek. The attack was furious, and many of General Crook's men were killed. The Indians simply faded back into the hills, joining their tribesmen at the Little Bighorn. General Crook returned to his base, so General Terry heard nothing about Crook's defeat until much later.

Major Reno came back from his scouting expedition to report that he had found a fresh Indian trail headed for the Little Bighorn Valley. "That's where I think the Indians are," he told Custer.

"That makes sense," Autie answered, looking at his map.

This called for a conference with General Terry. When Custer reached General Terry's headquarters, he found Colonel Gibbon there too. General Terry listened to Autie's report, looked at the map, and made his decision.

Custer was to take his men—about six hundred soldiers plus Indian scouts—up Rosebud Creek to the southern end of the Little Bighorn Valley. Terry and Gibbon planned to reach the northern end with their forces by June 26. (It was now June 22.)

"If the Sioux are there," Terry said, "we should be able to crush them between us. But don't be greedy," he warned. "Wait for us."

"Good, General. I won't," Custer responded. This was the kind of action he had been looking for.

"Remember. We'll be at the northern entrance to the valley at dawn on the twenty-sixth," Terry said to Custer, "with cavalry, infantry, and artillery."

Gibbon and Custer then talked about how they could time their marching to arrive at the valley on the same morning.

"I've got a couple of fine scouts who know the land south of the valley," Gibbon said. "Maybe you could use them."

"I'll take them," Autie said gratefully. "Good luck, General."

"Good luck, Autie." Gibbon smiled, shook hands, and left.

The Seventh moved toward the Little Bighorn the next morning. There was no laughing now. This was grim business. They traveled light. No tents. No heavy supply wagons. Only a pack train of mules.

On they went, heading for the spot where the Bighorn River met the Little Bighorn. That was the southern end of the valley. The scouts reported that there were Indians only a day's march ahead.

Custer hurried his Seventh. He was always like a hound dog on the trail. Once he caught the scent, he wanted to keep on going. The Seventh was fresh and it could march fifty-five miles a day if it had to. Finally, on the morning of June 25, 1876, the Seventh reached the entrance to the Little Bighorn Valley.

The scouts had been sent ahead. To the left was a hill called the Crow's Nest. It overlooked the valley. Custer turned to his aide, Lieutenant Cook, and said, "Let's go up there and take a look."

They rode up the hill, and while Cook held the horses, Autie lay down to search the valley with his eyes. Not a sign of smoke. Not a sign of a pony herd. Of course, he could see only about half the valley, but he was satisfied. There was no sign of an Indian.

He and Cook went back to wait for the scouts. They weren't long in coming.

"There are a lot of Indians in that valley," one of them said.

"I can't see a sign of them," said Custer, peering into the valley. "And I've got good eyes."

"I saw one big village, must have been four hundred lodges. That could mean a thousand Sioux," the scout said. "And there's lots of forest cover there. Maybe twice or three times that number hiding."

"You're crazy," Custer said. "I don't see a sign of smoke."

"If you don't find more Indians in that valley than you ever saw before in your life, you can hang me," the scout said sturdily.

Bloody Knife came riding up fast, his face serious. "Many Sioux," he said. "It would take days to kill them."

"All right, we'll kill them," Autie said calmly.

Then he hesitated. General Terry had ordered him to wait until the morning of June 26 so they could attack together. But that was twenty-four hours away. Why not sweep the valley clear of Indians before General Terry arrived? These old scouts were too cautious. They saw Indians behind every bush. Probably weren't more than a thousand Sioux in that valley. And he had the

Seventh—six hundred veteran fighters headed by officers he'd trained himself.

It didn't take him long to make up his mind. He called his most trusted officers around him and gave crisp orders.

"McDougall, you take eighty-four men and bring up the rear with the pack train," he ordered. "Captain Benteen and Major Reno will each take three companies. Captain Benteen, you go west, scouting for Indians. Reno, you attack that village the scouts saw to the east. I doubt if there's anyone in it but squaws. I'll go down the center with Troops C, E, F, I, and L. That'll give me about two hundred and ten men. If you get into trouble, Reno, don't worry. I'll be there to support you. You'll be to my right; Benteen will be on my left."

"What do you aim to do?" Major Reno asked. Unlike Custer, he was a careful officer.

"What do I aim to do?" Autie exploded. "I aim to drive every Indian out of this valley."

And he set out to do just that.

18

☆　☆　☆　☆　☆　☆　☆　☆

INTO THE VALLEY

A commander doesn't often divide his regiment
into three separate units. But Custer was an old
Indian fighter. This is how he had always fought.
It had always worked before—why not now?

Huge, white-haired Captain Frederick Benteen
would hit the Indians on the left flank; Major
Marcus Reno would hit them on the right flank;

and Autie himself with his favorite troops would hit them in the center. Autie's column would be in the middle. Benteen would be about three miles to his left and Reno about two miles to his right.

The three columns formed quickly and began to march into the valley. Custer felt proud as he looked at the officers commanding his five troops. First Lieutenant Algernon Smith was in charge of Troop E; his old pal Captain George Yates was in command of Troop F; Captain Myles Keogh had Troop I; and Jim Calhoun was riding in front of Troop L. Naturally Custer himself rode with Troop C, commanded by his brother Tom.

Most of these men had swooped down on Black Kettle's village with Custer. They had been with him when he rescued the two white women from Medicine Arrow. They had fought the Sioux at Yellowstone River and had hunted in the Black Hills with him. They were good, experienced men who could fight with gun, tomahawk, or knife. Both young Bos Custer and the still younger Autie Reed rode with the colonel.

Out of the corner of his eye Custer watched Myles Keogh on the big gray horse Comanche. Only a week before Autie had been given this horse as a present. The big horse was filled with spirit. He took a lot of handling. But he was a great horse. However, Autie had Dandy and Vic. He didn't need another horse. Keogh's favorite mount had hurt his leg and was hobbling around the stockade. Autie decided to give Comanche to Myles Keogh.

"He's a lot of horse, Myles," Autie had said, laughing. "But you're a lot of rider."

"He's wonderful," Myles said, his eyes shining. "Comanche is the strongest horse I ever rode."

On they rode into the valley. Now they were alone—just a few more than two hundred of them.

And except for the fact that they all died, that is all that any first-hand witness has been able to tell of Custer's last battle.

But knowing the kind of man Autie was, it is possible to guess how he *might* have fought that battle.

Here is one possible version.

It was nearly noon, a crisp day even though it was June. A still blanket of silence hung over the whole valley.

But fifteen miles away old Sitting Bull was in his lodge getting reports. He had been getting them all morning. Sitting Bull was the supreme Indian commander. Every Indian warrior now took orders from the wise old chieftain. Sitting Bull knew exactly where General Terry and Colonel Gibbon were.

Crazy Horse was in charge out in the valley, but he took orders from Sitting Bull. Two Moons and Dull Knife were in charge of the Cheyennes. It was the same Dull Knife whom Autie Custer had once threatened to hang.

All the great Sioux warriors were hidden on the tops of the three ridges which ran almost the length of the valley. Gall, Bob-Tail-Bull, High Hump Back, Little Wolf, American Horse, and Walking Hawk were all chiefs in their own right. But on this fateful day they were all lieutenants serving under Crazy Horse, who took his orders from Sitting Bull.

Every move that Autie Custer made was seen by a thousand Indian eyes. When he left the Crow's Nest and decided to storm the valley with three columns, Crazy Horse knew it within minutes. He sent Walking Hawk hurrying to Sitting Bull's headquarters.

When Sitting Bull heard the news, he arose. "Tell Crazy Horse to divide the three columns. Decoy Yellow Hair away and then cut him off from the other two columns."

Walking Hawk touched the right side of his forehead with his left hand, in the Sioux salute to a chief, leaped to his horse, and headed for Crazy Horse.

Meanwhile, what was happening in the valley? Major Marcus Reno had been given orders to storm the village. He stormed it, but there wasn't even an answering shot. Autie had been right. This was a big village, but it was deserted.

Reno pushed on, thinking that Custer was not far away, ready to support him if he was attacked in great numbers.

Autie, hearing no firing from the direction of the village, probably thought that Reno didn't need his help, so he swung far to the right to circle a high ridge. Now he was separated from Major Reno by the ridge and from Captain Benteen by three ridges. Custer wanted to hurry to the far end of the valley. If there were Indians in the valley, that's where they would be. He beckoned to the men behind him and they spurred their horses, charging north, far away from Major Reno.

"Sioux!" Autie cried, pointing ahead. "After them!" There were indeed forty Indians, but they weren't galloping; they were trotting. Autie Custer should have known what that meant. He had known it at the Yellowstone River when he'd told Tom that it looked like a trick.

He should have known now, but his blood

was crying out, "Get them, get them!" and he lengthened the stride of his big brown horse Dandy. Bill Cook and Tom rode on either side of him. The forty Sioux trotted up a ridge and down the other side. Custer and his men were right behind them. As they topped the ridge, they must have seen a sight that chilled them.

The plain on the other side of the ridge was filled with moving figures, and the moving figures were all advancing. Here were more Sioux than anybody could kill in a day, as Bloody Knife had said. How many? A thousand? Two thousand? There was no time to count.

Custer wheeled his horse and cried, "Retreat!" Then he saw that there could be no retreat. A cloud of yellow dust was coming toward them from the rear; dust kicked up by the hard feet of five hundred Indian ponies.

"Off your horses!" Autie Custer shouted. The men of the Seventh flung themselves off their horses. They were on the top of a ridge entirely surrounded by Sioux on three sides. The Little Bighorn River was on the fourth. Being on top of the ridge gave them one advantage. They could fire down at the Indians storming up the slopes. But there was a disadvantage, too. Custer couldn't send a messenger to Reno or to Benteen asking for help. So the two hundred and ten grim-faced men knelt and trained their guns on the screaming Sioux.

Major Reno couldn't have helped anyway. He had also ridden into a trap. The deserted village had also been a decoy. Reno, always cautious, had continued to advance, sure that Custer was only a few minutes to the left of him. He didn't know that Custer had veered far to the right and was ten miles away. Now Reno and his one hundred and forty men were also fighting for their lives. But he had sent a messenger to Benteen and the scout had gotten through.

Captain Benteen was riding hard to help Reno. He had also sent a message to General Terry advising him that the situation looked serious.

Back on the ridge Custer's men were taking a horrible toll of the Sioux. The warriors came from all sides, riding up the slopes, firing as they came. They were easy targets, but there were so many of them.

"Crazy Horse!" Bloody Knife shouted, pointing toward a lean Indian wearing but a single black eagle's feather in the band around his forehead.

"Get him!" Autie cried. He aimed at the tall Indian, who came galloping up the hill, leading the attack. He rode Sioux fashion, bending over the neck of his horse, getting some protection that way.

As Crazy Horse rode he cried, "Eeeeeeeee . . . ahhhhhhh!" and a thousand Indian throats echoed, "Eeeeeeeee . . . ahhhhhhhh!" Tom Custer and Bill Cook took careful aim at Crazy Horse, but the Indian bore a charmed life.

Every man on the ridge now, including young Bos Custer, was pumping fire from his rifle, and the slopes of the ridge were a tangled mass of dead horses and dead Indians.

Even Crazy Horse knew that this attack had failed. He wheeled about, held up his left hand, and pointed down the slope. Obedient to his command, the warriors turned about and headed for the plain. Now they would regroup to form again.

Up on the ridge Autie Custer looked around him. His young brother Bos lay there, a bullet through his forehead. Jim Calhoun and Myles Keogh lay dead.

What were Autie's thoughts? Was he aware of the terrible fate in store for him and his men?

Later Custer's enemies pointed out that he had disobeyed General Terry by attacking the Indians on his own. His friends and supporters charged that Major Reno could have rescued

Custer but was too cowardly. (Major Reno was eventually officially cleared of the charge.) Many others blamed General Terry and his staff for not having a better idea of the size of the Indian force.

Who was right? Nobody will ever know for sure.

19

☆   ☆   ☆   ☆   ☆   ☆   ☆   ☆

CUSTER'S
LAST STAND

Back in his lodge, Sitting Bull was getting regular reports. Benteen had joined Reno and they were fighting their way through the circle of Sioux and Cheyennes that surrounded them. But Yellow Hair was still alive; Yellow Hair and his men still knelt on the ridge, firing as only they could fire.

"Crazy Horse says he has lost five hundred

men," said Walking Hawk, the scout, sliding off his horse to report.

"Yellow Hair must be killed," Sitting Bull said gravely. "Tell Crazy Horse we fight for the life of the Sioux. As long as Yellow Hair lives, he will be a danger to us."

Walking Hawk hopped back on his horse. But Crazy Horse didn't need any orders. He was reforming his hordes of vengeful braves. Although Crazy Horse was an Indian, he was a genius at cavalry fighting. So was Custer. Now at long last they were fighting each other.

But Crazy Horse had three thousand men under him. Autie Custer had started with just two hundred and ten. Now more than half his command had been either wiped out or put out of action.

Faithful Bloody Knife stood beside him. The next charge came. Again it was led by Crazy Horse. Autie took careful aim and fired. Then he who never missed was shocked to see that he had missed. His bullet had hit the horse and the pony faltered, then stumbled. Crazy Horse tumbled away, unharmed.

Within three seconds he had hopped on another horse. The Sioux had often said that no white man's bullet would ever kill Crazy Horse. The Sioux swarmed up over the ridge and now

rifles were useless. They swung their tomahawks, and Autie and Tom and Cook and Yates
and the rest fired pointblank with their pistols.

Thirty minutes before, a blanket of silence had
covered the valley. Now it was torn apart by the
wild war cries of the Sioux. By the terrified
screaming of wounded horses. By the sounds of
carbine, rifle, revolver fire. There were also tiny
shrill screams as bullets cut the air overhead.

Once more the attackers fled, at the orders of
Crazy Horse. Once more Custer and those who
lived could breathe easily for a moment. The
ridge was a scene of wild confusion. Dying Sioux
and dead troopers lay beside one another.

"How many left, Tom?" Autie cried out.

"About thirty," Tom panted, wiping the blood
away from his forehead. An arrow had plowed a
furrow through it, but he scarcely felt it.

"What about young Autie?"

"He's dead," Tom said.

Autie gripped his brother's shoulder.

"There is only one hope for us, Tom," he said.
"We've got to fight our way out of here. One
more charge will finish us all."

"But how?" Tom asked.

"Down the slope to the river," Autie said. "If
we can make it and get across the river, we may
be able to stand them off until help comes."

"I'll tell the men," Tom said.

"Will help ever come?" Autie breathed to himself.

Reno and Benteen had fought themselves clear. Their casualties had been heavy, but now they were together.

Farther south messengers had told General Terry the story. But he was still forty miles away. In desperation he ignored the trail and cut across the mountains and the rivers. Anything to save Custer and the Seventh. But would he be in time?

Up on the ridge the thirty men were ready.

"The river is two hundred yards from here," Custer told them. "We will run one hundred yards and then drop to the ground. They will have seen us by then and will attack. If we beat them off, we'll run the other hundred yards, wade the river, and hide behind the boulders on the other side. They may think it is a trick. They might wait to see what happens. They may not know how many of us have been killed. Are you ready?

"Now!" Autie cried, leading the wild pell-mell run down the slope. They ran forty, then fifty, then sixty yards, and not a shot was fired. Then came the wild, shrill "Eeeeeee . . . ahhhhhhh" from the throat of Crazy Horse. Seventy . . . eighty . . . ninety . . . a hundred yards and they flung themselves down on the ground, panting. They formed a circle and their guns blazed.

"Here they come!" Autie cried.

Indians came from all sides, and the guns of Autie and his men never stopped firing. Crazy Horse had read Custer's mind. He knew that Autie and his men were trying to make for the boulder-strewn ground across the river. He sent a hundred men to stay between Custer and the river. He told them to dismount and fire at the little band of thirty. He would attack from one side. Rain-in-the-Face would attack from the other side.

Custer, kneeling there, understood Crazy Horse's plan, and he knew now that he could never reach the river.

"We'll have to fight it out here," Autie told Tom. "This is our last stand. And we'll take lots of Sioux with us," he added grimly.

And then they came. Yates fell under the blow of a tomahawk. Crittenden fell with an arrow through his heart. Riley clutched his side and dropped. Now the Indians who had been stationed between the river and Custer attacked. Custer was surrounded on all sides. His men were twenty against a thousand. Autie Custer and his brother Tom died as they had lived— together.

20

☆   ☆   ☆   ☆   ☆   ☆   ☆   ☆

THE ONE SURVIVOR

Sitting Bull was in his lodge. Scouts came constantly with new reports. It was all over, finally. Reno and Benteen hadn't been able to get through. They had managed to get to a bluff, where they were safe until Gibbon and Terry arrived.

Crazy Horse rode up furiously, threw himself

off his horse, and cried out joyously, "We have slain Yellow Hair and all his men. We have won a great battle, Sitting Bull."

"We have won a battle," Sitting Bull said gravely, "but we have lost a war. Yellow Hair has beaten us. Oh, yes, we killed him, but he and his men killed hundreds of our greatest warriors. The white man can find men to replace the soldiers who died on the ridge. Can we replace the braves they killed?"

"We killed many of Reno's men and many of Benteen's men," Crazy Horse said.

"True," Sitting Bull said, the wisdom of the ages on his old wrinkled face. "But what now? More soldiers will soon be here. Can we fight them now? They are like the leaves of a big tree. The wind and the frost kill the leaves, and the next year, lo—there are new leaves on the tree."

Crazy Horse sat down wearily. He bowed to the wisdom of Sitting Bull.

"You are right, Great Chief," he said slowly.

They found Autie Custer the next day. Gibbon and Terry had arrived. The Sioux, victorious but wounded almost to death by the number of their casualties, had fled. They would never be a serious threat to the white man again.

Terry's soldiers found Custer and all of the

two hundred and ten men who had died on the ridge and on the slopes of the ridge that was to become known as Last Stand Hill. There was not a single survivor.

But wait! They heard the faint whinny of a horse among the dead. A veterinarian who had come with General Terry rushed to the horse. It was Comanche, the big gray Autie had given to Myles Keogh only a week before. They cleaned Comanche's wounds and bandaged them, and then the big horse got up slowly.

They led him away reverently. Comanche was the only survivor of Custer's last stand. General Terry gave an order that no man should ever throw a saddle over Comanche. The horse would live out his days at Fort Lincoln, and thousands would come to see him.

Only Comanche knew the real story of Custer's Last Stand. But Comanche never said a word.